Cognitive Behavioral Therapy
CBT

Learn the secret techniques to overcoming negative behavioral, Anxiety, Depression, Eating disorder

by

David Wallace Beck

Table Of Contents

Introduction

Cognitive Behavioral Therapy (CBT) is a therapeutic tool that is used to help people who suffer from addictions, anxiety, depression, and other mental health disorders. Some of the key features of this type of therapy are ease of use, a rather hands on approach, and it can be custom tailored to the needs of the individual.

CBT has grown in popularity through the years despite the fact that there are those who criticize it. It has grown so much that there are now plenty of CBT variants that deal with different types of conditions. Some of these types are not actually therapies themselves but they are more utilized as training tools.

Some of the most popular types of CBT will be covered in this book. It should however be pointed out that no matter how many types of CBT there are the main idea and philosophy behind all of them is that changing maladaptive thought patterns will change a person's behavior. And that is at the core of the practice.

This book covers the trade secrets and techniques used in Cognitive Behavioral Therapy for treating depression, eating disorders, anxiety, and other negative behaviors. The content goes over several delivery protocols along with examples on how you can practice them on your own.

It should be pointed out that not all CBT forms can be

practiced on your own. In fact, there are a variety of delivery protocols in this type of therapy. Each method of delivery will have its own pros and cons. But it should be emphasized here that a face to face meeting with a CBT trained therapist is highly required. Doing so will increase your chances of success in the course of treatment. Why is that? We go over the reasons why in detail in this book.

CBT today is a conglomerate of different types of therapies. They are united by a common thread – the use of a cognitive behavioral approach to treatment and training. Some types of CBT are better suited for certain conditions such as the following:

- Internet addiction
- Eating disorders
- Smoking cessation
- Gambling addiction
- Mental illness prevention
- Mood disorders
- Psychosis
- Schizophrenia
- Anxiety disorders

Different types of CBT can be customized for different conditions. In this book we will go over Mindfulness-Based Cognitive Behavioral Hypnotherapy, Stress Inoculation Training, Moral Reconation Therapy, Structured Cognitive

Behavioral Training, Cognitive Emotional Behavioral Therapy, and Brief Cognitive Behavioral Therapy. That is not a complete list of the different types of CBT in practice today but those are some of the most common ones that you will find.

CBT is effective no matter which type because it is able to provide three important key elements for patients. They include the following:

1. It helps the patient regain that sense of self-empowerment. That means that they are again able to take responsibility for their own thoughts and behaviors.
2. CBT also emphasizes self-efficacy. That means clients are empowered to choose what they want to become.
3. The final aspect of CBT is that it teaches people how to live and focus on the here and the now.

CBT is not completely without fault. As a practice it does have its drawbacks. That is also the reason why there are critics of this therapeutic approach. Here are some downsides to name a few:

- You need to commit yourself to the process. It requires a lot of cooperation. If a patient lacks commitment, then chances are the therapeutic program might fail.
- CBT may not work well for people with a complex mental health need. People with learning disabilities may not be able to grasp the concepts being taught through CBT practice. This is due to the fact that CBT

takes on a more structured approach that would seem too difficult for some patients.

- You may experience an increase in anxiety since you will be made to face the very thing that causes you stress and depression.
- Some critics argue that causes of the behavioral problem may not exactly be addressed in actual CBT practice
- CBT is more focused on an individual's problems with themselves. Other problems with a wider scope such as relationships with families and coworkers may not be efficiently addressed.

In this book we will go over the criticisms leveled against CBT, its pros and cons, as well as its scientifically proven approach. This book takes on a rather balanced approach going over what you can get from it and where it may be lacking. The goal is to give you all the angles in order to help you to decide if this is the right form of therapy for you.

Chapter 1: Cognitive Behavioral Therapy—A Description

For many years what people thought of sessions with a therapist was pretty much the same thing. You will undergo some form of psychoanalysis. In that approach you will have to meet with your therapist several times a week. But you can schedule the meetings once a week.

These frequent visits sometimes last for months. At other times they last for years. And that is one of the things that made the whole process difficult especially for everyone today in the modern age. Everyone is just too busy and can't really put in the time to work on their emotional and mental health.

That was how therapies went for the better part of the 20th century. However, things started to change in the 1970s. Newer and different approaches and modes of therapy were introduced back then. A lot of them were short term with some lasting only a few weeks and others just a few months.

By the latter end of the 70s it was reported that there were almost 200 different kinds of therapies that people could subscribe to. The number of therapies continued to grow with some getting nods from distinguished scholarly and medical bodies while some were dismissed.

In 2010 it was reported that there are now 400 to 500 types of psychotherapy that were being put into practice. Of course the exact number still needs to be verified. The sheer number of psychotherapies shouldn't make you hold your breath. You see when you compare them one to another only a handful of them would turn out to be effective and scientifically based.

On top of that only a few of them are actually highly effective when it comes to solving the actual problems. These are the actual problems why people go out to seek the help of a therapist. They include stress related problems, phobias, anxieties, and depression.

One of the most effective of these modes or types of therapy is CBT or Cognitive Behavioral Therapy. It is actually one of the few types of psychotherapy that have been referred to as part of the gold standard. That means it is one of the best forms of therapy for the above mentioned conditions that people are actually struggling with.

Support for CBT

Cognitive Behavioral Therapy is backed by more than 300 clinical trials since its inception. Our understanding of its effectiveness is based on the collective knowledge of the medical experts who conducted these studies themselves. These are actual clinical trials and a lot of them have also been peer reviewed, which means the procedures and methods used in the studies have been verified by an independent party to avoid any bias when drawing conclusions.

These studies were conducted by personnel from institutions like the National Institute for Health and Clinical Excellence in the UK and the National Institute of Mental Health in the USA.

In these clinical trials it has been demonstrated that CBT can be effective for people of any age and background. It has been found to be effective for people coming from different cultural backgrounds, and different levels of education. It can be utilized as individual one on one therapy sessions and also as group therapies.

What Is It Exactly?

CBT is a form of psychotherapy, which means that it is a mode of treatment that does not use medical means (i.e. the use of drugs and medicine). It addresses psychological problems and at the same time it also boosts a person's happiness.

The approach used by CBT is through the modification of thoughts, behaviors, and emotions. This approach does not probe a patient looking for emotional or psychological wounds that are seen as the root causes of a person's internal conflict. That is actually the approach taken by traditional Freudian psychoanalysis.

Cognitive Behavioral Therapy instead focuses on possible solutions. It will encourage you to challenge any distorted views and also alter destructive behavioral patterns. The main idea or philosophy behind CBT is that our perceptions and thoughts tend to be a huge influence on our behavior.

Our perceptions of what is real and what is not can get

distorted whenever we feel distressed. This is supported in many cases though it may not always be true for everyone. People have various tolerances for stress. These thoughts and perceptions that do not reflect reality are called cognitive distortions. We'll go over that later in more detail.

That is why in CBT the goal of the therapist is to help you identify the thoughts that are harmful. You will learn how to assess if your current thoughts are a depiction of reality or if they are not. In case you are able to decipher that your thoughts and perceptions do not really reflect reality then you will be taught how to challenge these thoughts and also how to use different strategies so you can modify them and achieve more productive and positive thoughts.

3 Phases of Cognitive Behavioral Therapy

You experience a continuous cycle of negative feedback when you are afflicted with general anxiety disorder, depression, obsessive compulsive disorder, post-traumatic stress disorder, and other similar conditions. These things usually require some form of direct intervention so that this negative feedback cycle will stop.

Take away that direct intervention a person's fears and distorted beliefs will continue to bother the individual and eventually will dominate the mind. Sooner or later it may also threaten to rule a person's life.

Remember that human mind is wired to pay close attention when one's fears actually become real or something close to it (even though how remotely it may see). That means even the most remotely related negative events in a person's life can reinforce negative thought patterns.

The good news is that CBT has provided a way for psychiatrists and other health workers to break that cycle of negative feedback. After that vicious cycle has been disrupted (and hopefully broken) positive and more constructive thoughts can enter. Healthy thought patterns can then be inculcated by the human mind.

The unhealthy thought cycle must first be broken or at least interrupted before you can let healthy and positive thought patterns to return. CBT is often implemented in 3 phases, which include the following:

1. Healthy coping skills
2. Being mindful of your inner thought patterns
3. Identifying and exposing yourself to the things that trigger your stress response

Phase 1: Relaxing Exercises and Coping Skills

CBT sessions will usually have you start learning how to cope with stress. Your therapist or a session facilitator (in case you are joining a group therapy session or training) will help you learn different CBT skills. We'll cover these skills in a later section of this chapter.

These coping skills will allow you to challenge any negative beliefs that you may have formed. This will help you rewire your system and move you along the path to recovery. These CBT skills can be used anytime and anywhere but it will require some practice before you can use them well.

You may already know some of these skills already but you just don't know how to correctly use them. For instance, you may have already noticed that breathing or deep breathing to be exact has helped to calm you down one time or another.

However, you don't know which part of that breathing pattern was actually able to help you get relaxed. A lot of us attempt it by inhaling slowly and then exhaling as fast as we can. Well, that's what we've seen boxers and MMA fighters do in between rounds, so sometimes we think that's the way to do it.

However, you should understand that anxiety will cause you to hyperventilate. Breathing deeply can help a bit but that is not exactly the right breathing pattern. We'll go over that and the other details when we cover CBT skills later in this chapter.

Phase 2: Mindfulness Skills

Related to deep breathing exercises is the meditation practice called mindfulness. This type of meditation has been around for hundreds of years and it has been used by Buddhists to bring practitioners to a relaxed sense of self.

Mindfulness skills can help you address your current state of mind, which is the second phase of CBT. Once you become aware of your inner feelings and thought patterns, you can begin to challenge them stop the negative thoughts from invading your subconscious.

You can challenge all that negativity using positive statements. You will then learn how to establish more affirming beliefs about yourself that help build you up. Some of the things that your therapist can help you with will include tools like a journal and exercises that reinforce a positive outlook.

Phase 3: Inoculation

There are a lot of things that can trigger a stress response in a person. Different individuals will have different sets of stress triggers. These triggers can be anything such as certain places, noises, experiences, events, smells, and even things that you see.

These triggers can incite mental health symptoms. Some of them can also cause people to react with anxiety and depression. Inoculation or trigger exposure will help you overcome stressors and their associated triggers. It's like getting shots that will help boost your immune system. You are exposed to minimal amounts and weaker forms of a virus that helps your body build an immune response. You will also learn how to build your own defensive response as you grow more accustomed to stressors and their triggers.

What are Cognitive Distortions?

As it was explained earlier, the term cognitive distortion refers to any thought or perception that is either irrational or exaggerated. It also refers to thought patterns that are influenced by anxiety, depression, and other psychosocial factors.

Cognitive distortions cause people to see and perceive reality rather inaccurately. This negative outlook is referred to by experts as negative schemas or schemata for short. Schemata are one of the key factors of emotional dysfunctions. It is also a sign of a person's poor well-being.

One thing usually leads to the other. That means negative thinking patterns will always lead to negative emotions. Cognitive distortions lend to a negative overall outlook especially during difficult circumstances. They can also cause an anxious mental state as well as depression.

Types of Cognitive Distortion
The following are the main types of cognitive distortions. Note that they are actually types of automatic thinking. They are thought patterns that people formulate almost habitually. They are to be distinguished from logical fallacies which one usually arrives at after some deductive reasoning. Cognitive distortions are more than just realizations or a pattern of reasoning.

- *I am always right*

In this type of cognitive distortion one believes that being wrong or in some cases committing a mistake is something that is totally unthinkable or impossible. It does not necessarily mean that a person believes that he or she is incapable or committing mistakes or is absolutely infallible.

This cognitive distortion is where one actively tries to prove that one is correct both in both thoughts and actions. It doesn't matter if is actually wrong or right—even though a patient believes he is wrong then he will still try to prove that he is right.

The priority in this type of cognitive distortion is none other than self-interest. The feelings or position of others is irrelevant. Even if others are correct and one is wrong actually wrong it doesn't matter. What matters is that one is able to prove that one is right.

- *Disqualifying the positives*

In this cognitive distortion any positive event will be disqualified. The only things that need to be acknowledged are the negatives.

- *Blaming others*

With this type of cognitive distortion, the priority is putting the blame on other people. One would rarely acknowledge any mistakes that one has committed. This is the opposite of another distortion which is called personalization.

If you have this distorted thought pattern, you will almost always and almost immediately hold other people responsible for any emotional distress that they may have caused you or someone else. It doesn't matter if the harm was intentional or not. It also doesn't matter if it was only some kind of negligence. The important thing is to pin the blame down on other people and not on the self.

- *Jumping to conclusions*

If you have this type of distorted thought pattern chances are that you immediately create negative preliminary conclusions about things even if there is very little evidence for it or even none at all. Most of the time the conclusions are negative but there are times when the conclusions that are drawn are positive.

There are two sub-types of this cognitive distortion, which are the following:

1. Fortune telling – here you try to predict the outcome of certain events. The predictions for the events are usually negative. For instance, you come to a job interview but then you see that there are other well dressed and smart looking applicants. You immediately draw the conclusion that you will not get the nod during the interview even though it hasn't even started yet.

2. Mind reading – here you try to infer or deduce the other person's thoughts. Again the prediction is based some superficial behavior or non-verbal cue which actually has no bearing on the subject.

A lot of times the person with this kind of cognitive distortion will take actions and measures against the negative condition being suspected. It is done without even bothering to ask the person directly.

For example, a guy comes over to pick up his date but he believes that she wasn't really up to it; maybe she was just coaxed into it by her friends. This is due to the fact that she wasn't really enthusiastic about it when he asked him out. And so the guy immediately concludes that she doesn't really want to go out with him.

Therefore he goes about it without any gusto. That is because he believes that it is nothing more than a pointless exercise. And he also comes to the conclusion that perhaps he is also wasting his and her time.

- **Mental filtering**

Our minds are usually hardwired to see the negative. This is actually a defense reaction that we have developed. We suspect and emphasize danger, hard times, and other negative aspects of the things we experience more than the possible positive aspects.

However, those with this kind of cognitive distortion have a greater focus on a situation's negative aspects. The belief or perspective is that if something does not conform to beliefs that one has already held on to then it is something negative. That is the kind of filter that we will try to alter using Cognitive Behavioral Therapy.

- **Fallacy of fairness**

Now, this is not a logical fallacy but it is more of a fallacious thought pattern that everything in life should be fair. A person who has this cognitive distortion will tend to get angry when he or she perceives something is unfair. That person might even do something to correct what is perceived as unfair.

- ***Fallacy of change***

Again this is not a logical fallacy. A person with this type of cognitive distortion will resort to measures of social control. They will use such means necessary in order to make others cooperate with them.

- ***Emotional reasoning***

This cognitive distortion puts a lot of weight on one's feelings regarding certain subjects. Usually the feelings that are used to test and judge situations are negative. Again, the emotion that the patient feels does not match reality.

For instance, one person who has this cognitive distortion fears flying. He therefore concludes that flying via airplanes is no less than a truly dangerous way to travel. You can show him statistical data about how much safer are planes compared to cars and he would still not believe you.

His emotions are his rule of thumb. If want to convince him then you must help him overcome this cognitive distortion first. One of the best ways to do that is via CBT.

- ***Dichotomous reasoning***

This is the kind of cognitive distortion where one believes that there are no gray areas. They believe that there is only black or white, good or bad, yin or yang. Some even view things in life in extreme terms. The verbiage they use often describe things as being absolute such as all, never, everyone, and always among others. They use such terms when they are misleading someone or when they are lying about something.

- ***Personalizing***

This is a type of distortion where one attributes to oneself the responsibility for certain things. It can be about either something positive or negative. The result of such attribution is either praise or blame. Nevertheless when you investigate such claim that person had no direct control or influence over the reported event or incident.

- ***Overgeneralizing***

In this type of cognitive distortion, one will usually make hasty generalizations even if there is insufficient evidence. This is a pretty common distortion and sometimes everyone can slip into it once in a while. One who has this type of cognition will often draw very broad conclusions from whatever evidence they can gather no matter how inconclusive it really is.

For instance, if they experience something bad happening during a certain event they would think that trying it again will always lead to the same result. For example, a man went to the gym but he saw how unfit he was when he compared his physique with the other guys in there.

Plus, none of them were really that welcoming. He never set foot in a gym again since that time. He concluded that all gyms are the same – a place filled with guys who are so full of themselves. It is a place where they look down on people who have waistlines above 40 inches.

- *Exaggeration and Minimization*

You've heard of the expression "making mountains out of molehills." This is exactly that. People who have this cognitive distortion will put a lot of weight on the negative than on the positive. They exaggerate the negative and minimize the negative.

There are also people who undergo depression that tend to over exaggerate the positive characteristics of other people while at the same time are exaggerating their own negative features.

A subtype of this cognitive distortion is called catastrophizing. This means a person looks at things in the worst case scenario possible. It doesn't matter how unlikely their outlook is. Situations that are actually uncomfortable are seen as something that is impossible and/or unbearable.

- *Labeling and Mislabeling*

This is a kind of over generalization where instead of admitting that an event or act was nothing more than coincidence or an accident (i.e. something beyond one's control), one takes credit for it and attributes it to one's own trait or character.

CBT Skills and Delivery Protocols

In Cognitive Behavioral Therapy patients are taught and trained to build a set of skills that will equip them for dealing with the issues that they are facing. These CBT skills enable patients to become more aware of their emotions and their thoughts. These CBT skills are also the same delivery protocols that your therapist will use to help you into recovery.

In the process they will learn how their behaviors are influenced by their emotions and their thought patterns. The goal is to help people improve how they felt by focusing change on their behaviors and dysfunctional thoughts.

Note that in CBT the process of acquiring these skills is often collaborative. There should be another helping hand to guide you along the way until you acquire the necessary skills to change your thought patterns, mindset, and behavior.

What makes CBT unique from other forms of talk therapy is the fact that it focuses and requires skill acquisition and the assignment of homework for the individual. The therapist does more than just sit down with the patient and discuss issues and then just offer advice.

We will go over some of the skills that you can learn in CBT in the next section. Note that your therapist will guide you through these skills. Note however that some of these skills can be self-taught or something that can be learned on your own.

Skill #1 – Psychological Education

You may have heard of the phrase "educate before you inspire." That is representative of the approach in CBT. A therapist will not just offer advice right off the bat after some evaluation. An important first step when it comes to overcoming stress (or any other psychological problem for that matter) is to learn more about the said condition. This process is called psychoeducation.

Learning more about the psychological issues that you are going through helps you understand the process that will be involved in your treatment. It will also give you comfort knowing that you are not alone in the fight against the specific condition that you are going through.

You will learn that there are countless others who have gone through the same issues and have been successful in their endeavors to overcome it. It will also be a great help if your family members also learn more about the said problem as well. They will be the ones who will be with you most of the time. For a lot of people, understanding the nature of their condition is already a significantly big step towards eventual recovery.

For instance, if you were suffering from a form of panic attack, your therapist will begin by discussing with you what a panic attack is and what it is not. The important thing here is to dispel any misconceptions about the condition so that you are better able to help yourself and allow your family members to provide the appropriate support that is needed.

You will learn that a panic attack is something that is obviously uncomfortable. It is also quite alarming due to the symptoms that one feels at its onset. However, you will also learn that a panic attack isn't really something deadly. It isn't even that dangerous and that it is only temporary.

Psychoeducation is not confined to the therapist's office alone. You can learn more about your condition by reading books from the library. You can also gather information from the internet provided that you are getting it from reputable sources. This is an important step albeit the first step in the process of Cognitive Behavioral Therapy.

Skill #2 – Improving One's Mood by Increasing Activity Levels

When your mood is low it can affect you in several different ways. It can impact your body's physical levels as well as your thoughts. Your mood can influence your behavior. In fact when our mood is low we would rather stop doing things—we say we're not in the mood. And a lot of times we lose the mood to do the things that we used to like doing.

An example of the effects of low mood on a person is when one becomes less active. People also at times withdraw from their daily activities that they need to perform. They also withdraw from hobbies and other interests.

A common phenomenon is that when people feel like they

want to do less what they stop doing are the things that they used to find enjoyable. They will remove these activities from their weekly schedule—sometimes saying that it's only a temporary thing. But in the end they end up quitting the very thing they used to love doing. Withdrawing from these activities feed one's low mood because you reduce your chances to interact with other people—especially people who share similar passions and interests.

It also feels easier to do nothing and thus people will feel like they just want to do less. By simply increasing your activity levels you are able to break free from this rather vicious cycle. Your therapist and other people who support you will help to encourage you to become more active. It is not just being active per se. You need to create some form of structure (i.e. a scheduled and programmed approach) in your activities.

Your therapist will help you schedule activities (or you can schedule them yourself). You will also be reminded and urged to follow through with your schedule. There will also be an assessment at every CBT session to follow up on your progress and find out how your activities are affecting your emotions.

It won't be like your therapist will just wait until you feel like you're in the mood to do something. Your therapist, group leader, or some other CBT facilitator will help you create your activity schedule and categorize each of them. There are 3 main categories of activities that you should engage in, which include the following:

1. **Routine Activities**: these are activities that you do regularly on a day to day basis. They include the usual stuff like showering, cooking breakfast, fixing your bed before going to sleep, brushing your teeth, taking a shower, doing the laundry, going to work, and watching TV among others. These are routine activities—some of them are necessary while others are not but you can do them and you usually just do them every day.

2. **Necessary Activities**: these are activities that we have to do whether we like them or not. We have to do them because there will be consequences if we do not. Some necessary activities may be done routinely while others are not. These activities include cleaning the house, going to work, and paying the bills.

3. **Pleasurable Activities**: these are the activities that we really like to do. They are the ones that we are truly interested in. They may include playing videogames, sports, visiting friends, fishing, golf, swimming, and others.

Note that there will always be activities that can belong to more than one category. Don't fuss about categorization too much when you make your activity plan for each week. And it doesn't have to be a really tight schedule. The goal here is to create a balanced increase your activity levels. There should be enough routine, necessary, and pleasurable activities that you will be doing each day.

How to Increase Your Activity Levels

1. Make a list of activities. Include routine, necessary, and pleasurable ones in your list. Make sure to include things that you used to do and love but have stopped doing.

2. Create a hierarchy of the different activities in your list (the ones you added in step 1 above). The most important ones (and the most difficult ones) should be at the top of your list while the least important ones should be at the bottom. Don't forget to add a classification for each activity as described earlier.

3. Use an activity diary or some other journal to make your daily task schedule. Make sure to mix things up with necessary, routine, and pleasurable activities. You can start your day with smaller and easier activities at first at least to get you started.

4. Build up your schedule by adding more difficult activities in your list. Make sure to include a time stamp when you should be doing each activity. Make the description of each activity detailed. It can look something like this:

"8 AM – go jogging with Mindy at the park for 30 minutes"

5. Get up and go. If you have to drag yourself to get it done, do it. If it will help to involve someone to get things going for you (i.e. "Mindy") then do it. Do the activity with a friend or family member. That way you have some support and encouragement. Remember that an activity schedule/diary is just a list—it won't be effective if you don't do something about

it.

6. Review the activities that you have done during the week. Review each activity that you managed to accomplish. Evaluate how you feel about the increase in your activity levels. How did it affect your mood? Find out what other activities you can include in your schedule/diary for the following week.

Is there something new that you would like to try? Ask yourself what particular thing about certain activities made them more difficult thus making you want to do them less. Include your thoughts and you can add notes about who you think can come with you with the other activities you have on schedule.

Sample Activities List

Routine Activities

1. _____
2. _____
3. _____
4. _____
5. _____

Necessary Activities

1. _____
2. _____

3. _____

4. _____

5. _____

Pleasurable Activities

1. _____

2. _____

3. _____

4. _____

5. _____

Activity Hierarchy List

Hardest to easiest list:

1. _____

2. _____

3. _____

4. _____

5. _____

6. _____

7. _____

8. _____

9. _____

10. _____

11. _____

12. _____

13. _____

Sample Activities Schedule

		Monday	Tuesday	Wednesday
Morning Activity	What			
	Where			
	When			
	Who			
Afternoon Activity	What			
	Where			
	When			
	Who			
Night Activity	What			
	Where			
	When			
	Who			

You can add more activities in your list or you can make your list more detailed or simpler than the one shown above. Make sure to indicate the time of the activity and who might be there to accompany you.

Finally, at the end of the week you should grab your journal or diary and review each activity that you have written down in your schedule. Write down your thoughts and describe your mood after getting all of that stuff done.

Skill #3 – Relaxation Techniques

Learning how to relax your body and your mind is part of CBT training and therapy. Two of the physical symptoms of anxiety and stress are muscle tension and shallow breathing. They can also be signs that one is depressed.

That is why it is important that you should be aware of these symptoms. In CBT you will also be taught relaxing exercises that will help you overcome these symptoms. We will go over some of the strategies and techniques that you can use to relax in a later section.

Relaxation Response

What is the stress response? When a person is overwhelmed by stress the body gets a chemical dump that prepares it for maximum defense. This flood of chemicals produced by the human body (i.e. hormones) prepares the person for lifesaving situations. The body is prepped for defense and also to act quickly.

However, when your body is prepped for stress every day like that, it takes a huge toll on you. Human beings aren't designed to cope with stress 24/7 and the huge hormonal dump will wear us down physically and also emotionally.

The fact of the matter is that stress happens to everybody. No one can avoid it. But the good news is that we can avoid its otherwise detrimental effects. All we have to do is to learn to create what is known as the relaxation response which counteracts the body's fight or flight response to stress and danger.

It's like learning to put your foot on the breaks and not get the pedal to the metal sort of thing. These two responses are polar opposites of each other. You naturally know how to do one (i.e. the fight or flight response). Now you will have to train how to perform the other (i.e. the relaxation response) thus creating an equilibrium within you.

What happens during a relaxation response? They involve the following:

- The heart rate goes down
- Breathing becomes deeper and slower
- Your blood pressure begins to stabilize
- There is an increase of blood flow to your brain
- Your muscles start to relax

If you want to know what the fight or flight response is like, all you need to do is state the opposite of all the five points mentioned above. You will be taught several ways to trigger this relaxation response when you attend CBT sessions.

Other than getting you calm, relaxation techniques will help you focus and eventually increase your energy levels. It has been found to increase productivity levels, boosts motivation, heightens problem solving abilities, relieves pain, and combats illnesses.

Anyone can perform the relaxation techniques that will be

described below. However, there are other things that can be done to produce the effect of a relaxation response. But they will require the services of a professional such as a therapist or an acupuncturist. Some relaxation techniques can be performed with the help of an app on your phone while others come in the form of audio downloads. We'll cover the different modes of access that you can use for Cognitive Behavioral Therapy in a separate chapter.

How to Choose the Right Relaxation Technique

Note that there is no such thing as a relaxation technique that will work for everyone. It will always be different for everybody. That means you should try different methods as they are described below and of course you can find other relaxation techniques through other sources. Your therapist may even suggest something new that might just work very well for you.

You should find the ones that best suit your lifestyle. But more importantly they should be techniques that resonate well with you—which means the technique produces that relaxed state.

How you react to stressors will also help to determine which techniques will best suit you. Do you react to stress with a flight response? Is it a fight response? Or maybe it is an immobilization response?

- **The immobilization response** – have you ever seen a deer freeze when a car's headlights flash in its eyes? A lot of people freeze when they are confronted with something dangerous—like a bully, a mugger, or maybe a rabid animal. If this is your normal response to stress then you should find activities that allow you to focus your attention and sensations on your limbs. Anything that helps you stay in touch with your arms and legs so you can become more aware of the freeze response and counteract it.

- **The flight response** – this response entails getting spaced out, withdrawn, and getting depressed when stress finally wears down on you. If this is you then it is recommended that you use techniques that stimulate your nervous system. Examples of which include power yoga, mindfulness, massage, and rhythmic exercises.
- **The fight response** – some people tend to get angry and agitated when they get stressed. These folks will better respond to techniques that tend to get you calm. Think along the lines of the superhero character the Black Widow calming the Hulk-that kind of thing. Some of the techniques that you might want to try includes guided imagery, deep breathing, and muscle relaxation.

Important Note: some people need either social support or some alone time when learning relaxation techniques. Take time for some personal evaluation. Ask yourself, do you crave for some solo time? Then techniques that can be done alone such as progressive muscle relaxation and meditation are for you. Do you crave social support? Are you better motivated by group interactions? Then class settings group activities maybe the best way for you to learn the relaxation techniques that will be described below.

Deep Breathing Exercises

The focus in deep breathing is to use cleansing breaths. This is a simple yet powerful way to obtain a relaxed state. On top of that it is also very easy to learn. It does not require any specialized training since everyone instinctively knows how to breathe deeply.

Deep breathing is considered as the cornerstone of a lot of relaxation techniques. It can also be combined with other techniques such as music and aromatherapy. There are a lot of different breathing techniques and you can learn them via apps and audio/video guides.

Important Note: most of us are familiar with breathing from the chest. This is natural however, if you want to stimulate that relaxed state, you need to learn how to breathe from the belly, which is called belly breathing. This type of breathing stimulates the vagus nerve, which is responsible for the relaxation response. Stimulating this nerve lowers your stress levels, helps to reduce blood pressure, and it makes your heart rate go down as well.

Sample Deep Breathing Exercise:

1. Sit comfortably on a chair

2. Keep your back straight

3. Place one hand on your chest

4. Place another hand on your stomach

5. Breathe in through your nose

6. Notice which hand is rising as you breathe in deeply

7. If the hand on your chest is moving more than the hand on your stomach then you should do some adjustments to their movement

8. Breathe in but this time let your belly bulge and try not to expand your chest that much as you inhale

9. Remember to inhale through your nose and exhale through your mouth

10. Inhale enough air to make your abdomen rise and fall

11. Count slowly from 1 to 5 when you inhale, hold your breath, and then exhale as long as you are able, and then hold your breath for 3 more seconds. Repeat the breathing pattern after that.

Progressive Muscle Relaxation

Progressive muscle relaxation requires a two-step process. This isn't a really complicated process so don't let the name of this relaxation technique intimidate you. All you will be doing is to tense and then relax muscle groups in your body—that's it.

Surprisingly, when you that you will discover that you tend to create muscular tension without knowing it. After going over this exercise you will feel that you are no longer as tense as you were when your stress levels went up. What's more is that you can combine this technique with deep breathing exercises to further increase the relaxing effects.

Important Note: if you have a history of muscle spasms then you might want to consult with your doctor first before trying progressive muscle relaxation. This is also true for people who have current physical injuries and back problems.

Sample Progressive Muscle Relaxation Exercise

1. Loosen your clothing
2. Remove any tight fitting garments, socks, shoes, gloves, jackets, and others
3. Remove any jewelry that you are currently wearing
4. Breathe in and out deeply for 2 minutes
5. You can actually do this exercise either standing or sitting—but since you want to relax then it would be best that you take a seat and get comfy
6. Put your attention to your right foot
7. How does your foot feel?
8. Next, increase the tension on the muscles of your right foot
9. Squeeze them tight as if you are in a body builder competition showing off your muscles
10. Hold your tensed muscles for 10 seconds and then release
11. Relax the muscles on your right foot

12. While in this relaxed state breathe in and out deeply for 1 minute

13. Repeat the same steps but this time do it on your left foot

14. Remember to do deep breathing while relaxing your muscles for 1 minute

15. Repeat the steps described above contracting different muscle groups in your body and then relaxing them

16. Remember not to contract/tense up the other muscles that you are not working on

17. After working on your feet do the same steps but this time work on your right calf and then your left calf

18. Next do the same for your right thigh and then followed on the left thigh

19. Next do your hips and buttocks

20. Next do it on your back muscles

21. Follow that up with your chest muscles

22. Right arm and then left arm

23. Right hand and then left hand

24. Neck

25. Shoulders

26. Finally do the same exercise on your facial muscles

Body Scan

Body scan is a type of meditation and this technique is also used in mindfulness practice as well. Again, don't let the name of this technique intimidate you. The name of this technique is rather descriptive than anything.

All you are doing is focusing your attention on one part of your body and then moving it to the other ergo the scanning part. The pattern will be very much like what is described in the previous exercise (i.e. progressive muscle relaxation).

Instead of flexing and the muscles of each body part, you will just pay attention to each of them. Remember that this is more meditation than exercise. You can do the body scan meditation first thing in the morning before you get up and off the bed.

You can just remain lying down and start your day with a five minute meditation. Of course you can also do it any time of the day especially when you feel that the stress is already too much. Just find a nice comfy bed to lie on (or any surface that has some kind of matting will do).

Body Scan Exercise

1. Find a comfy bed or matted space
2. Make sure that you can be alone in that place for at least 5 minutes
3. Lie down on your back
4. Keep your legs straight
5. Place your arms at the sides of your body
6. Keep your legs and arms relaxed
7. If you have any muscles that seem tense take the time to relax those muscles

8. You can do this meditation either with your eyes open or closed—it's all up to you

9. As you lie there focus on your breathing

10. Pay attention to how the air feels as you inhale and exhale it

11. Remember to breathe slowly – you can count 1 to 4 as you inhale and exhale or not – it's all up to you

12. Just remember to pay attention to your breathing—this is the important part

13. Breathe in and out 10 times paying attention intently to the sensations that you get with each breath.

14. Next, shift your attention your toes. Start with the ones on your right foot and then move to your left foot

15. Make sure to spend at least 2 to 3 minutes focusing on each body part.

16. If at any moment certain thoughts or memories invade your body scan and tries to break your concentration just observe it

17. Watch as the memory or feeling or even fear passes away—they always do, they come like a storm but they just pass away

18. Continue your focus on your ankles, then go up to your knees and legs

19. Go up to your thighs, hips, back, stomach, chest arms, and all the way to the head

After completing a body scan relax and just enjoy the silence.

Allow the stillness to soak into you and give your soul a taste of peace. Now it's time to stretch and get up to start (or go on with) your day.

Mindfulness Meditation

After doing the body scan exercise above you have already had a taste of mindfulness meditation. Mindfulness allows you to focus on the present and it puts you square into the present moment. It empowers you to switch your ability to focus not in the past or to worry about the future—it switches your focus on the present, where it should be.

This type of meditation has been around for centuries and people have been using it to relieve stress. Today it is used as a tool to overcome anxiety and depression. There are many kinds of mindfulness meditations. Some of them will make you focus on a single repetitive action.

That repetition allows you to focus on the present. It will allow you to release any thoughts, fears, and other feelings that have been bothering you. You can apply this principle to any other activity—walking, eating, running, jogging, or even just sitting in the train until you get to your designated stop.

Basic Mindfulness Meditation Example

The body scan exercise described earlier is already a fine example of mindfulness meditation. Here is another simple kind of mindfulness meditation that you can try:

1. Find a quiet place where you can be alone and remain undisturbed

2. It should be a place that is free of distractions and interruptions

3. You can sit on a chair that is comfy enough or you can also choose to sit on the floor—it's all up to you where you find it comfortable

4. Use a point a focus—examples of which could be the sensation of the movement of air as you breathe in through your nose and out through your mouth.

5. Another point of focus is could be something external like maybe a candle that you have lit from a distance that you can focus on.

6. Another point of focus that you can use is a word that means a lot to you. All you have to do is to keep saying that word over and over like a mantra.

7. As you try to concentrate on that focus point you will notice that distracting thoughts and memories will enter your mind

8. You should also not worry about how well you are doing at concentrating at that singular point of focus.

9. When these things try to bring your focus away and even if they do succeed forgive yourself and then bring your focus back to the focus point that you were using earlier.

10. There is no need to fight these thoughts and

11. memories—just observe them without judging them as good or bad. Observe them and watch how they come and go. Just bring your attention back to your point of focus each and every time.

Tai Chi and Yoga

Yoga has gained popularity in recent years and tai chi still has a following. Some may think that these are martial arts but they are actually more of a healing art than anything. Yoga as you may have already seen in social media and perhaps on YouTube involves stationary poses as well as gentle subtle movements. It is often combined with deep breathing to further facilitate a relaxing and meditative state.

Note however, that yoga may cause injuries if you perform the movements incorrectly. That is especially true of its advanced poses. The best way to get started in yoga is by attending yoga classes. In that setting you will have an instructor to guide you along the way, which helps to prevent injuries from happening.

Private lessons of course will cost more but at least you have someone supervising you directly. Once you have learned the basics and are already confident in your ability to perform yoga poses then you can move on to yoga videos, some of which are actually free.

Types of Yoga for Stress Relief

There is no specific type of yoga that will be required for CBT.

Your therapist can recommend certain types for you. Note that almost all forms of yoga will end in a relaxation pose, which is great for stress relief. Your therapist might recommend yoga that emphasizes gentle stretching, deep breathing, and slow steady movements.

Here are a few types of yoga that you might want to investigate apart from what a therapist might recommend:

- **Power Yoga** – this is the type of yoga for fitness buffs. If you love working out or if you like to focus on physical fitness as well then this might be the one for you.

- **Hathat Yoga** – this is a kind of yoga that gives you a reasonably gentle way of stretching. It challenges your body a bit since the poses are a bit more difficult than the basic poses but it will help keep in the zone and enter that relaxed state.

- **Satyananda Yoga** – this is the traditional form of yoga. If you have gone through the yoga basics then your instructor may have already given you the fundamentals of satyananda yoga. This is the type of yoga that makes use of more gentle poses which is great if you're after that meditative state. This is the type of yoga that is better suited for beginners since it also espouses deep relaxation techniques as well. If you're just after stress reduction then this might be the type of yoga for you.

So, What about Tai Chi?

Have you seen the animated movie Kung Fu Panda? Do you remember the soft flowing circular movements that they show there? A lot of that is Tai Chi. Is it a kind of kung fu? Well, yes, and no.

You see Tai Chi was originally created for self-defense. However, as the centuries went by people have found that the movements of this art also help to keep the body healthy especially when you grow older. It is also particularly good at relieving stress.

Some people call it as meditation in motion. You see you will be doing a lot of gentle moves. The big difference between Tai Chi and Yoga is in the execution of the movements. Yoga is more about holding a pose and maintaining a specific set of postures for the body. Tai Chi on the other hand looks more like a slow flowing dance, which of course looks like Kung Fu.

If you're older or maybe you aren't that flexible anymore (or maybe you have a problem with mobility) then Tai Chi might be a better fit for you. If you are okay with some challenging poses and you can handle some stretching then why not try yoga.

Guided Imagery

Another name for guided imagery is visualization. Again, this is a variant of traditional meditation. The main idea behind guided imagery is to focus your mind visualizing or imagining a scene where you are feeling total and complete peace.

It doesn't matter if you have actually been to that place or not. Choose the setting that is the most calming and peaceful for you. It can be a favorite place when you were a child or it can be the perfect peaceful place that you can imagine. The important thing is that it is a place where you feel at peace.

You can practice guided imagery with the help of a therapist and you can also do it with the help of a phone app or an audio or video recording. You can do this exercise in total silence or you can play your most soothing music. Some people listen to recordings of a forest while others do their visualizations while listening to the sound of the ocean waves.

Guided Imagery Sample

1. Set a timer for 5 minutes
2. Close your eyes
3. Imagine your chosen restful place
4. Picture every detail in your mind
5. Add details like what you see, how it feels, what smells are there, and if you imagine food or drinks imagine their taste as well.
6. Imagine it as if you were actually there and not just like you're watching something on TV or in the movies.
7. Fine tune the details – where are you at? What are the things around you? How does it feel when you move from one spot to the other? What do you hear up close

and also from a distance? How does the air feel like there? Are there any distinct smells about?

8. Enjoy the relaxing atmosphere in that place. Let it all soak in.

9. Look around your special place and be free to roam around

10. Picture the details of the immediate surroundings.

11. When the timer goes off slowly open your eyes

12. Try to recall the feelings while you were there in that place that you visualized

13. Breathe in deeply counting from one to ten

14. Exhale slowly until you have emptied out all the air in your lungs

15. Breathe normally and feel the peace that you have gained and let it carry you through the day

Note that there will be times when you will lose focus and zone out of this guided meditation exercise. That is okay. It happens to everyone. You may even feel strange things like heaviness in your limbs and back. You may also experience some kind of muscle twitching. Sometimes you get so relaxed that you just yawn. Remember that these are very normal and they happen from time to time during this kind of meditative exercise.

Rhythmic Movement

Rhythmic movement can be combined with mindfulness meditation. It can be anything that allows you to move to a certain rhythm—again you don't need rocket science to do this. Now, you might think that there is nothing relaxing about exercise but you may be a bit surprised how rhythmic exercises can bring you in the zone.

Repetitive movement can get you in the flow. It's not the exercise itself that brings you to a relaxed state. The exercise is only your gateway to bring your mind to focus – when you focus on repeating that movement over and over again it brings your mind to that relaxed state, and that is what you are actually looking for.

Examples of rhythmic and repetitive exercises include the following:

- Dancing
- Running
- Rowing
- Walking
- Climbing
- Swimming

So, how do you maximize the effects of rhythmic movements? Here's how.

You get the maximum effects from rhythmic movements when you add mindfulness meditation to them. What you need to do is to be fully engaged in what you are doing, paying attention to how your body is feeling, and leave your worries and concerns behind.

For instance, when you focus on the rhythm of your steps when you go jogging, you turn off the thoughts and worries you have about work, home, and all the other things that preoccupy your mind.

Pay attention to each step. How does your breath feel? Are you feeling tired? Then you need to reduce your running pace. Maybe switch to a speed run instead. Oh so you remember that bothersome coworker that gossips all day?

Well, okay, let the thought pass by and then go back to monitoring your steps. Do you feel stronger? You think you can go back to a full jog? Have you already caught your breath and have a second wind? Then go try it.

What you need to do is to focus on your run, rowing, walking, swim strokes, and what not. Forget the world around you and focus on what you are doing at the moment. Get into the zone and leave the world behind.

After you're done with your rhythmic exercise notice how relaxed you feel. Notice how it would seem that a huge weight has been lifted off your shoulders. Do you feel like you're ready to take on the challenges of life? Yes you are—you've been energized. That is the power of rhythmic movements combined with mindfulness.

Getting a Massage or Do a Self-Massage

There's no arguing it. Getting a massage is a great way to get relaxed and revitalized. A day at the spa usually gets anyone refreshed. However, you can't always go for a full spa session and it can be a bit expensive depending on the type of treatment you want to get.

However, you may not know that you can also get the same level of pain and stress relief by doing some self-massage. Well, if you're trying to get to the hard to reach areas then you can get your spouse or another family member to give you that massage. You can then trade massages, they massage you first and you can massage them after.

How to Give Yourself a Massage/Trade Massages

To massage yourself or somebody else you can use gentle chops of the edges of your hands or by lightly tapping the area to be massaged with cupped palms. Another way to do it is by using your fingers to apply pressure on muscle knots and other areas of the body using circular motions.

1. Start by using a kneading motion as you apply mild pressure on your shoulders and at the back of your neck.
2. After that make a loose fist and then lightly hammer down at the back and sides of your neck.
3. Place your thumbs at the base of your skull and then move them around using small circular motions on that area.
4. Massage your scalp using the your fingertips going from the front to the back and then after that going to the

sides

5. Massage your temples using small circular motions with your thumbs for 30 seconds.

6. After that gently slide your thumbs going to the center of your forehead as you apply some slight pressure.

7. After your thumbs meet at the center of your forehead use your other fingers to line up at the center and press down gently. Drag your fingers from the center of your forehead going to your temples. Apply gentle pressure as you slide them along the way.

8. Press your thumbs against the joints on your jaw—do this gently

9. Make small circular movements as you do.

10. Now, move your thumbs along your jaw line as you make circular movements until both of your thumbs meet at the center near your chin.

11. Use your middle fingers to massage the bridge of your nose in the same way pulling them along the lines of your eyebrows stopping at your temples.

12. Finally, breathe in slowly counting 1 to 10 and then exhale slowly until all of the air in your lungs has gone out. Repeat this breathing technique for 1 minute. And now you're done.

Skill #4 – Graded Exposure

Graded exposure is a way for you to face your fears or whatever it is that causes you stress. It would be best that you go over these exercises with a therapist. When people are faced with something that they fear (or anything that causes them stress), we go over what is called the fight or flight response.

It has been discussed earlier in this chapter. The "fight" part is when we ready ourselves to respond quickly and of course fight back. On the other hand, the "flight" part is when our bodies and minds prepare to protect ourselves from a coming onslaught.

Graded exposure prepares us to manage such a natural response by desensitizing us from our fears through exposure to stressors. You see, avoiding or escaping from a stressful situation may remove the anxiety really fast.

However, when the stressor or cause of that anxiety returns, we still experience the same level of anxiety as before. In consequence we haven't really resolved the issue. We have only avoided confronting it.

In CBT, graded exposure aims to equip you to face the things you fear and eventually reduce the amount of anxiety that you may experience. The solution, ironically, is to stay in that stressful situation albeit in increasing degrees of intensity.

Graded exposure involves a person staying in that situation that causes him or her to be anxious. You see, there are levels of stressors—some being more stressful than others. For instance, a man may have a problem with public speaking.

After investigation, a therapist finds out this guy was really afraid of being the center of attention. That is why one of the things that he fears the most is giving a presentation to his coworkers. The root cause is the former and problem that he reported was the latter.

The therapist works with him and exposes him to different grades of the thing that he fears. They create a list of things related to the fear of being the center of attention. The top of the list is the thing that the man feared the most—giving a presentation at work in front of his peers.

They identified and wrote down related things that he feared, which you will find below. Remember that at the top of the list is the thing that he feared the most, followed by the next most frightening thing, and so on.

Here was his list:

1. Giving a presentation at work
2. Making the same presentation in front of his family
3. Commenting on his wife's cooking
4. Asking details about a product at a store
5. Putting on clothes that make you stand out in a crowd
6. Practicing a presentation in front of a mirror

What the therapist will do is have that man do number 6 on that list. After he has become comfortable with that they will then simulate or practice number 5. And then they will progress upward on that list until finally the guy is ready to try number 1.

Note that this process is not a quick fix. There is no guarantee that after going from numbers 6 to 2 that he is automatically confident enough to do number 1. He may even fail along the way and will require encouragement and support.

You can actually do this on your own. List down related things that you are afraid of then arrange them from the most frightening one to the least stressful one. Work your way up your list from the least frightening/stressful to the most stressful one.

Key Points to Graded Exposure Success

- Your fear must be gradually confronted
- Your exposure to the thing that you fear should be long enough to allow stress levels to go down. That means a treatment session should last long enough until you are only about 50% afraid of the stressful condition.
- Your exposure to stressors needs to be repeated several times—about 4 to 5 times each week.
- Exposure exercises should be free of distractions. That means you cannot use breathing exercises, relaxation techniques, music, and other coping mechanisms. The goal is to expose you to your stressors at maximum levels until you become used to them.

Graded Exposure Sample Steps

The following is a sample on how to go over a graded exposure exercise.

1. Create a list of things that you are afraid of (i.e. things

2. that cause you stress).

3. Arrange them from the most to the least feared item (i.e. your anxiety ladder)

4. Face/practice the least feared activity/item on your list over and over again until you are only about 50% afraid of it.

5. Repeat the practice up to 5 times this week.

6. Do not use any distractions etc.

7. Write an evaluation on your journal/diary.

8. Repeat everything from step 3.

This anxiety ladder method slash graded exposure is also useful for other challenges that you may be facing. Some have used it to overcome the things that they worry about. Worrying of course is kind of related to fears and worrying also causes anxiety.

Skill #5 – Challenging Your Negative Thoughts

Another skill that your therapist will introduce to you is challenging your negative thoughts. This skill will help you manage unproductive and non-beneficial thought patterns. When people are overcome with anxiety their thoughts tend to follow an unrealistic and negative pattern.

In CBT negative thoughts and negative thinking patterns are referred to as Negative Automatic Thoughts or NATs. Remember that in CBT philosophy human thoughts influence emotions and behaviors.

Although people generally understand that their NATs may not be true it is going to be very difficult to differentiate them from facts. A person's low mood and anxieties can take over and they are very powerful influences.

Here are a few examples of what can be considered NATs:

- They must think I am stupid
- I will lose my job if I arrive late
- Everything is going wrong
- I can't do anything right
- She will never really like me

How to Challenge Your NATs

When you want to challenge your negative thought patterns, you will have to go through 3 necessary stages. They include the following:

1. Catching your thoughts
2. Look for evidence
3. Find an alternative thought that is based on actual evidence

Catching Your Thoughts

The first stage is called catching your thoughts – or catching your negative thoughts to be exact. This first stage can be the most challenging phase for anyone especially for those who have made it a habit to focus on the negative.

Your therapist will spend a lot of time with you to practice catching your NATs. You will also have to categorize your

NATs as well. You see, some NATs will cause you more stress than others. The ones that cause you a lot of anxiety are called Hot Thoughts.

You will also identify how "hot" (or how distressing) each thought is usually from 0% to 100%. Your therapist will go over this with you during the course of this CBT skills training.

Probing Questions

The following are probing questions that you can ask yourself when you challenge your negative thoughts. Take a minute to answer each of these questions and answer as honestly as you can:

- Where were you?
- If it is true then what does it say about you?
- What were you doing?
- What was the worst thing that crossed your mind?
- Who were you with?
- What were you telling yourself?

Reminders When Catching Your NATs

Negative thoughts may sometimes be difficult to spot especially when you have been used to them for quite some time. Here are a few important reminders.

- These negative thoughts will always sound reasonable at the time
- They usually do not occur in a logical series or in steps
- They do not come out of the process of careful thinking

- NATs can occur in both images that you imagine and words that you say
- They come along rather quickly after events that you notice
- They are usually very specific and they are often short.

Focus on the Evidence

After catching your NATs the next thing you need to do is to look for and focus on the evidence or lack thereof. You will find that your negative thoughts will hardly have any evidence or basis for it if any.

Focus on the evidence and then you can better challenge the negative thought—there's no evidence for it right? Then there is no need to worry about it. It also opens avenues for more balanced and realistic thoughts. It will also help to brighten your mood. Factual evidence is a more powerful tool to dispel negative thoughts and doubts because you have something you can hold on to that actually makes sense.

Finding an Alternative Thought That is Based on Evidence

This can actually be a separate skill in CBT but we'll just include it here. The third and final phase to challenging your NATs is to find alternative and evidence-based thoughts. You will do this after establishing the fact that there is little to no evidence for the NATs that you were harboring.

Remember that you are not trying to come up with just the opposite of your negative thoughts. Note that CBT is not actually concerned about positive thinking. That is not the goal. The goal is to make people go back to making realistic and more balanced thoughts.

Think of an alternative thought to the one that is bothering you. Ask yourself if there are other ways to look at a situation. You can also put yourself in someone else's shoes—how would they look at this situation? With each alternative you come up with try to find evidence for it. If there are grounds for that alternative then try to gauge if it is a better and more realistic option or thought.

Here's an example on how to do that.

Problem Thought: you feel that everyone hates you

Extreme Alternative Thought: you feel that everyone loves you

Balanced Thought: there are people who may not like you but there are also others who do.

In this example let's say that you feel that everyone hates you. It may seem very plausible to you since negative thoughts or NATs are usually automatic. However, after examining it you may think of one or two people who actually do not like you but there are plenty of other people who have appreciated you or maybe have complemented you.

The complements and acts of appreciation are the evidence to the contrary of the NAT. You focus on those and hang on to those things. And then after some further thinking you will also notice that there maybe a few people who do not like you.

As you can see, you are getting more realistic. You move away from the belief or thought that everyone hates you to a more balanced thought that there are people who also like you and appreciate you. But you do not discount the possibility that maybe there are those who may really not like you.

That is more realistic because there will always be someone who will not like you. But that does not discount the fact that there are those who do like you. This is what CBT aims for. It's not just plain old positive thinking. The thrust is to go back to that balance in thinking and feeling. And the way to do is to go look for and validate your thoughts based on the evidence that is available.

Opinions change and everyone is entitled to their opinions. But opinions are not always facts. Check your negative assumptions and see if they have facts supporting them. Go with the facts and look for your balance.

Skill #6 – Problem Solving

Sometimes the things that cause you stress and worry are actual problems that you need to resolve. That means you need to deal with difficulties in a practical and methodical way. A logical problem solving approach will be as follows:

1. Identify the problem
2. Identify all the possible solutions
3. Evaluate the pros and cons of each option
4. Arrange the options into a hierarchy from best option to

5. least beneficial option
6. Select a solution that works best for you
7. Make a plan on how to execute the solution (create detailed steps if necessary)
8. Put the plan into action
9. Review the results

Problem Solving Sample

Let's say you need to pick up your kid from school tomorrow but then your boss told you that he will interview you for a coming promotion so you will need to stay an hour or two longer at work. That means you won't be able to pick up your kid from school.

This of course can make you worry since you can't be at two places at the same time. It can also cause anxiety and of course you will need help to solve this problem. You can't just do positive thinking here and you can't just choose positive thoughts over negative thoughts. This time you really need to work out a solution.

Putting the problem solving thoughts that we have outlined earlier, here's what you do.

1. Identify the Problem: I have an interview with the boss and I also have to pick up my kid from school. I can't be at 2 places at the same time.

2. Identify Possible Solutions and Evaluate Pros and Cons: After much thinking you come up with a few possible solutions, which include the following:

- Ask your wife to pick up your child (but she might get angry if you ask her that coz she's tired from work too and she might demand that you should do your own share caring for the kid). But this is the easiest option and she might also like the good news about your coming promotion—so that might ease things up.

- Ask one of your friends to pick up your kid. This is a quick fix and it shouldn't be a problem. However, they may feel like you are forcing them, which will strain your relationship. It may also not look good to the wife and she may get upset as well. On top of that some of your friends are unreliable and they may get late picking up your kid or they may also be a bad influence to your child.

- Ask your boss if you can reschedule the interview. Your boss might say yes, but it will not make a good impression on him. It may even cost you the promotion, which would greatly help your family financially.

3. Arrange Options from Best to Worst: so, here's your list of options from best to worst:

    a. Ask your wife to pick up the kid

    b. Ask your friends to pick up your kid

    c. Ask your boss to reschedule the interview

4. Select the best solution: after checking out your list you go for option "a"

5. Plan How You Will Execute Your Solution: the plan

is to cook dinner for the wife tonight. After she has had dinner and is already feeling relaxed and cozy tell her that you have an interview with the boss tomorrow and will be getting a promotion. And then you tell her that you will not be able to pick up your kid. Ask her if she can pick up your child tomorrow after school.

6. Execute: cook dinner, make it a bit special. Wait for the best time to tell your wife. And then tell her. She agreed and now you can go and go on with your interview tomorrow.

7. Evaluate: the night after before going to bed write on your journal. How did everything go? Was the interview a success? Write everything down.

Things don't always work out as you want them. What if your wife couldn't pick up your kid because she too has an important thing at work? She could have and would be willing to do so if only you had told her sooner. Make a note of that— you should tell people in advance if there are things like this.

If that is the case then you move on to your next solution—ask your friends. The good news is that one of them is free but he is willing to pick up your kid on one condition—you get him free beer this weekend. Besides that, his kid is in the same school so it wouldn't be a problem since he always picks up his kid every day after work.

But what if that didn't work out? You couldn't find anybody. That means option "b" didn't work. You are left with your final option then. You will then have to for option "c" and talk to your boss. You should explain your situation honestly—or maybe you can ask him to just adjust the time (maybe pick up your kid first and then bring your kid back to work with you so you can have the interview?). Your boss could be a reasonable guy.

Skill #7 – Get Enough Sleep

When people are under stress they don't sleep well. Believe it or not, sleeping well at night can be one of the best things that you can do for yourself when you are experiencing a lot of stress.

A common myth is that people need exactly 8 hours of sleep every night. But evidence shows that the amount of sleep you need varies. And the more important thing is the quality of sleep rather than the amount of sleep.

Your therapist will go over this and other details with you. But here are a few tips that you can do on your own so that you can get to it right away even before your therapist gets to discuss this with you:

Dos:

- Check if you have any medications that are interfering with your sleep
- Create a comfy sleeping environment
- Exercise regularly but don't do it before bed time
- If you can't sleep, get out of bed and do a relaxing activity and then when you're already relaxed go back to bed and try to get some sleep

- Go to be when you are actually tired
- Wind down before going to bed
- Always sleep at a regular time

Don'ts

- Don't make up for lost sleep
- Never sleep when you feel tired during the day (but you can take naps)
- Don't take in any caffeine 4 hours before sleeping
- Don't read a book, watch TV, or eat while in bed
- Leave your worries behind when you're under the sheets
- Stop worrying about not getting enough sleep

Chapter 2: History of CBT

CBT has its philosophical roots as well as roots and derivations from behavior therapy and cognitive therapy. In this chapter we will go over a brief retelling of the history of cognitive behavior therapy and the details about its roots and beginnings.

Philosophical Roots

There are actually several precursors to the principles and philosophies behind Cognitive Behavioral Therapy. In fact some of them can be traced to different philosophical traditions of the past. Some even believe that CBT has ancient parallels in Stoicism.

Stoicism was founded by Zeno of Citium back in 301 BC. It is a school of ancient Greek philosophy that eventually influenced the development of Western Culture as well as Christianity in general.

This ancient Greek and Roman philosophy aims to help people lead emotionally resilient and virtuous lives. It is a philosophy of personal ethics with the ultimate goal of achieving human flourishing.

Stoicism is one of several responses to the classic question put forward by Socrates: "how do you lead a good life?"

One of the philosophers of this philosophical school of thought was Epictetus. He believed that human beings can use logic to identify as well as discard false beliefs. He also believed that these false beliefs eventually led to destruction feelings and emotions, which of course is similar to what we see in the practice of CBT.

It was Aaron T. Beck who stated in his depression manual the very same thing. He says that the origins of CBT can be traced all the way to the teachings of philosophers of Stoicism. Other leading minds in this field such as John Stuart Mill and Albert Ellis also have stated the same thing alluding to other stoic philosophers and influencers.

CBT's Roots from Behavior Therapy

Note that the history of CBT is often described within what is called three waves. The first wave of Cognitive Behavioral Therapy is one that focused on operant learning as well as classical conditioning. The second wave of CBT then focused on information processing. Both the first and second waves of CBT are based on the initial premise that emotions, thoughts, cognitions, and psychological states affect and eventually will lead to dysfunctional behavior.

This is the process that is seen that happens to people who develop dysfunctional behavior. It is further believed that if you change or eliminate the causes of dysfunctional behavior the appropriate behavioral changes will take place. And then a third wave of CBT was developed. This third wave is fairly new and it is an attempt to increase the effectiveness of the first two waves. This third wave emphasizes experiential change strategies as well as contextual changes and they are evident in the strategies that are used in today's modern practice.

There is no mistaking that CBT has roots in behavior therapy. That is why if you look closely and do some comparisons, you will notice that the different types of cognitive behavior therapies (we'll go over them in a later chapter) are actually a group of related therapies.

CBT and these forms of behavioral therapies are referred to as the first psychotherapies that have an empirical basis. Now, when we say empirical what we mean is that these psychotherapies are based on actual scientific studies. That means their therapeutic strategies have been tested and scientifically proven to be effective.

It all began in the 1940s after World War II. There need for more effective psychotherapeutic interventions increased due to the huge number of war veterans who came home suffering from depression and anxiety.

The need back then was for a mode of therapy that was short term and also practical. The timing was perfect since during that time and decades before the Second World War, there was a build-up of scientific behavioral research. In short, prior to these events, psychologists have been doing a lot of research for decades.

They were trying to decipher how human beings learn how to behave. They were also trying to identify the how and why people react emotionally. This was the beginning of what is known today as behavioral learning theory.

Combined with the exponential need for psychotherapy services in the late 1940s, these efforts and rapid research became known as the first wave of behavior therapy or first wave CBT. They called it behavior therapy or behavioral therapy—both terms refer to the self-same thing.

This relatively new approach was different from the traditional forms of psychotherapy at the time, which was more Freudian based and is known as psychoanalytic therapy. Nowadays they are referred to as psychodynamic therapy. However, do take note that behavior therapy today is still used as a major part of other therapies. Sometimes people today use the terms behavior therapy, cognitive therapy, and cognitive behavioral therapy to refer to the same thing. But of course we know that there are subtle differences between them.

Modern CBT of course was derived from behavior therapy. The studies on behavior therapy began in the early 20th century. These studies on behavior therapy were then later merged with the studies related to cognitive therapy in the 1960s.

It was the studies published in the 1920s by Rosalie Rayner and John B. Watson on behaviorism that helped to start it all. From that point on therapeutic approaches that were more centered on a person's behavior appeared as early as 1924. Part of that was the work of Mary Cover Jones that focused on teaching children to unlearn their fears.

Another pivotal work in the development of CBT was Joseph Wolpe's studies on behavior therapy, which was based on conditioning and learning. Later studies on behavioral therapy followed but the techniques used in them were more based on classical conditioning.

Classical conditioning of course refers to the learning procedure where a stimulus is paired with another stimulus. The first one is biological and the second one is neutral. An example of a biological stimulus is food and an example of a neutral stimulus is a bell. The idea is to create a connection between the two stimuli to elicit a response.

In this example the ringing of a bell can be associated with the serving of food. Your mom or dad can ring a bell every time food has been set on the table. The children or everyone in the house can then come to the dining room for supper.

This can be repeated several times over the course of many months and then every time the bell is rung, it will produce the stimulated effect of anticipation of a meal. Since the people in the house have been conditioned to this stimulus, even though there was no actual food served on the table they will associate that sound with food. CBT of course takes this into account during therapy.

Joseph Wolpe also applied methods used in systemic desensitization in his studies. And as you may have already surmised, since it is discussed here in this book, certain approaches to therapy and a type of CBT called Stress

Inoculation Therapy (SIT) that also makes use of the same principles and philosophy. We will cover SIT in more detail in chapter 5 of this book.

Systemic desensitization is also called graduated exposure therapy. This type of therapy is mainly used in clinical psychology. It is actually effective in helping people overcome phobias and other similar types of anxiety.

This type of behavioral therapy also makes use of counterconditioning principles and techniques such as breathing and meditation. The procedure in graduated exposure therapy or systematic desensitization involves 3 steps:

1. Identification of one's anxieties and the creation of a hierarchy of stimuli
2. The learning and application of coping and relaxation techniques that will help them react better to the stimuli that create or produce anxieties.
3. Use the learned relaxation techniques to overcome the situations that have been listed in the hierarch of stimuli that have been listed in the first step.

Finally, beginning in the early 50s to the late 60s, experts introduced operant conditioning to the overall approach in behavioral therapy. For example, you can look up the work of B. F. Skinner with regard to radical behaviorism.

Operant conditioning is a learning process and it is also known as instrumental conditioning. In operant conditioning a behavior is either reinforced or punished. One of the goals of this process is to teach or help the subject of the study to learn. Reinforcement is used to increase the incidence of a behavior while punishment is used to decrease behavior. Reinforcement can either be positive or negative. An example of positive reinforcement is the adding of an appetitive stimulus (i.e. a pleasurable reward like giving a candy to a child) when the test subject does the expected behavior. An example of negative reinforcement is the presence of something noxious or scary. That thing which is noxious or undesirable (i.e. the punishment) will only be removed when the subject has performed the desired action or behavior.

The following diagram will help to explain the fundamental idea behind operant conditioning:

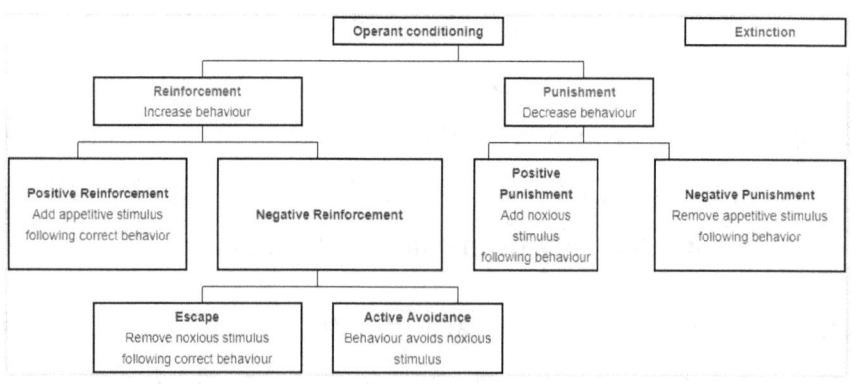

CBT's Cognitive Therapy Roots

The first wave of CBT generally speaking is that time during the development of CBT as a practice where the emphasis was on behavioral factors. However, experts on the subject could no longer deny the fact that cognition also had a powerful influence on a person's behavior. This was demonstrated in the works of Albert Bandura and Julian Rotter.

This so called second revolution in behavior therapy began when psychiatrists began actual empirical studies on how people's thoughts affected their emotions (i.e. cognition). And of course eventually it also had an effect on one's behavior.

At the time of its inception cognitive theory was a novel and revolutionary challenge to the original ideas of traditional behavioral therapy. That is also the reason why people called the second wave of CBT's growth and development as the cognitive revolution.

The second wave of CBT focused more on the thinking aspect of psychotherapy. This mode of therapy made more sense to mental health professionals as well as to the patients.

There were actually two cognitive sciences that contributed to the rapid growth and development of the second wave.

They are the following:

1. Social psychology
2. Computer science

Social Psychology – social psychology studies the complex ways of how people interact with one another and more importantly how they think about each other. It studies how people as a group or society behaved and how come societal groups viewed certain issues differently and especially about each other.

Computer Science – it may come as a strange thing for people when they learn that computer science (computer programming in particular) has any effect or bearing on psychology as a science and also as a practice. But it does have a profound effect.

Computer software and software programs led to the understanding you can create programming rules for human beings as well. It's not like you can create software that you can apply to human beings. But it was more the understanding of programming rules that can be used to influence human thinking and behavior.

These two studies added legitimacy to the cognitive side of the development of CBT. Now psychologists do not only have to rely on visible behavior of people during a study. They can make use of conscious thoughts and its role when assessing human behavior patterns. The combination of both behavior therapy and cognitive therapy eventually gave birth to what we know today as the modern version of CBT.

And this constitutes the second wave. However, it didn't end with a second wave—further growth and development in this mode of psychotherapy is yet going on in what is known as third wave CBT.

Third Wave CBT or Third Generation CBT

The merging of the first and second waves is known as the

third wave of Cognitive Behavior Therapy. In this third generation there isn't actually any new methodology introduced. What we have instead is an attempt to improve what has been introduced in both first wave and second wave CBT. However, it shouldn't come as a surprise in case another form of therapeutic approach will be added to what has already been introduced.

CBT as a psychotherapy practice turned 50 back in 2006. Of course we can't cover all the new types and subtypes of Cognitive Behavior Therapy in this book but we can only describe their similarities as well as some of their differences.

For one thing all types of modern day CBT emphasize empirical research. Just like traditional CBT they too acknowledge the importance of studying human behavior. On top of that they also acknowledge the important role of thoughts or cognitions.

So some would ask what if there are really any new revolutionary growths in CBT or are we just seeing more of the same? One area where third wave CBT therapists are looking into is a reexamination of current practices that are already in place. Remember that this new wave or generation of CBT is more concerned about fine tuning established procedures and practices.

For instance, CBT therapists are trying to determine whether controlling emotions and thoughts are truly a necessary part of solving a problem for a client or patient. This question and new approach has made CBT therapists to try new methods focusing on not just the content of a client's thoughts but also on their thought processes as well.

Traditional cognitive therapy is also going along this same course of action in its development. Third wave CBT today is placing greater emphasis on placing our thoughts in context and making sure that therapy sessions and practices react accordingly to human thought patterns.

In terms of the philosophical basis of it all, third wave CBT is veering away from the control of a person's internal experience. Today there is a more eastern approach to the subject of approaching a person's frame of mind. Somehow the goal or thrust is to make our behavior more adaptive.

The view is that the person's reaction to his own thoughts should be flexible and it should allow that person to live productive lives. It questions whether or not human efforts to control emotions and thoughts are using up too much of our own energy.

Now if you look at the landscape of therapies that are considered to be part of the third wave of CBT, you will see that there is a bit of a loose affiliation amongst them. All of these new forms of therapy make use of cognitive and behavioral therapy. That is a middle ground that they all have.

However, there are differences when it comes to application. We cover some of the most common types of Cognitive Behavior Therapy in chapter 5 of this book. However, it should be noted that it is not an exhaustive list of therapies that are considered third wave.

Here is a short list of therapies that belong to the third wave:

- Acceptance and Commitment Therapy (ACT)
- Brief Cognitive Behavior Therapy (BCBT)
- Mindfulness Based Cognitive Therapy (MBCT)
- Cognitive Emotional Behavioral Therapy (CEBT)
- Dialectical Behavior Therapy (DBT)
- Structured Cognitive Behavioral Training (SCBT)
- Behavioral Activation (BA)
- Moral Reconation Therapy (MRT)
- Functional Analytic Psychotherapy (FAP)
- Integrative Couple Therapy (ICT)
- Stress Inoculation Training (SIT)
- Cognitive Behavioral Analysis System of Psychotherapy (CBASP)

Note that there are more types of CBT that are not included in the list above. You can say that third wave CBT is slowly turning into a blanket term to refer to all therapies that are cognitive based psychotherapies.

All of the different types of CBT have become a blending of behavior and cognitive based elements. They also combine a variety of technical and theoretical foundations of the practice.

Chapter 3: Medical Uses

CBT today is incorporated into medical practice. In fact it is used as part of the overall treatment for many types of conditions, such as:

- Post spinal cord injuries
- Substance abuse disorders
- Anxiety and depression associated with fibromyalgia
- Schizophrenia
- Psychosis
- Personality disorders
- Chronic lower back pain
- Eating disorders
- General depression

CBT and Pediatric PTSD

It should be noted that there is no single treatment that can be used to address every case of post-traumatic stress disorder. CBT is only one of the many options and techniques used to treat this condition (i.e. childhood PTSD).

There are plenty of research and studies that have been conducted on the effectiveness of CBT for patients with this condition. However, despite all that research a review of medical literature on the subject shows that only a few of these studies were actually just randomized. That means there is a need for more clinical studies in this regard.

However, even with the limited meta-analysis that is available today, it is still suggested that CBT can be helpful in treating PTSD. It can address rule breaking behaviors, aggression, and other related symptoms. Studies have shown that CBT can also be useful either as a separate form of treatment or as a combination treatment for substance abuse disorders.

CBT and Anxiety Disorders

If you suffer from an incapacitating phobia, unrelenting worries, obsessive thoughts, and panic attacks then you may be experiencing anxiety disorder. CBT is a form of treatment that a clinician can offer to you. Other types of related treatment may also be recommended such as exposure therapy and others. These therapies and other related techniques may help you conquer worrisome thoughts and lower your anxiety levels.

CBT is one of the most widely used therapies for a variety of anxiety disorders. You will learn how to examine thoughts that contribute to fear and anxiety through cognitive therapy. Through behavioral therapy you will also learn how to examine your behavior with regard to situations and other factors that trigger an anxiety response.

Challenging Negative Thoughts

Part of the treatment for anxiety through CBT is a process

called challenging negative thoughts (also referred to as cognitive restructuring). Here are the steps used in that process.

1. **Identify Negative Thoughts** – situations are usually perceived as being more dangerous than they really are. For example, someone who has germ phobia may be afraid to shake hands with people even though it is perfectly safe.

2. **Relaxation Techniques** – after identifying negative thoughts that are unrealistic, you will be taught a variety of relaxation techniques that help moderate the body's physiological functions. These techniques will help you control your breathing, heart rate, and muscle tension.

3. **Hypnosis** – your therapist may include hypnosis as part of your overall treatment. Hypnosis will bring you to deeper state of relaxation. While in that state the therapist will use a variety of techniques to help you face the fears that you have identified and view them in a new and less challenging way.

Other techniques may also be used by your therapist such as exposure therapy and systematic desensitization. This part of CBT training will be best performed with the guidance of a dedicated clinician. You may perform the steps described in chapter 5 of this book regarding systematic desensitization but we do not guarantee any dramatic results without professional aid.

Problem Gambling Treatment

CBT has been demonstrated in various studies to be an exceptional tool to help patients overcome problem gambling. The short term and intensive nature of CBT helps patients to focus on achieving their goals and also to prevent the incidence of any potential relapse.

The following elements may be utilized by a clinician to help you address this habit:

- Assessment
- Planning of a course of treatment
- Establishing a therapeutic alliance
- Goal setting that is values based and other collaborative efforts
- Learning behavioral and cognitive interventions
- Planning and executing such plan to prevent future relapse

A therapist will help you overcome beliefs, habits, thoughts, and other cognitive distortions about gambling. Some of these cognitive distortions may include wearing the right shirt, bringing a lucky item, gambling at certain times, and plenty of others.

Once a person has been made aware of his cognitive distortions, the therapist can help the individual to challenge such beliefs. That client will be trained how to trace the origin of such a poorly framed beliefs. The discrepancies in those wrong beliefs will be used to compare the client's beliefs with reality. The goal of this part of therapy is to help patient see that there is no connection between their winning or losing with the cognitive distortions (aka gambling beliefs).

Once the patient realizes that next step in therapy is to implement techniques that will help them overcome their gambling urges. Notice that the beliefs are addressed first before there is anything done with the urges that the person feels. This is then followed up by plans to prevent any possible relapse in the future.

An important key in administering CBT for problematic gambling is identifying the reasons for gambling. According to clinical experience, determining this and role it plays as a coping mechanism against challenges that the patient is dealing with is vital in the recovery process.

Inventory of Gambling Situations

One of the tools that your therapist might use is called the IGS or Inventory of Gambling Situations which was developed by the Centre for Addiction and Mental Health (CAMH). IGS is a self-report questionnaire that is designed to identify the situations where a patient may be at risk for returning to gambling habits. The information that can be gathered through this questionnaire can also be used by your therapist to formulate a treatment plan that is specific to your needs in order to prevent a relapse from occurring.

10 subscales are included in the IGS to help therapists to identify certain triggers as well as gambling patterns in different areas such as:

- Confidence in one's gambling skills
- Winning and chasing after losses
- Worrying about debts
- Need for excitement
- Social pressure
- Pleasant emotions brought about by gambling
- Testing one's personal control
- Gambling urges as well as temptations to gamble
- Dealing with conflict with other people
- Negative emotions

IGS can also help therapists produce a client profile. This profile will help you identify possible risks in many different situations. This profile will also suggest ways to cope with the gambling triggers. IGS is available online and it can also be downloaded as an app on Google Play [click here]. A therapist may use this or another psychometric evaluation tool to help patients with problem gambling.

The Role of Cultural Perceptions

As a patient discusses their feelings toward their gambling

problems one of the key factors that can influence the treatment plan is the role of cultural perceptions that a person may have. Note that there are cultures and subcultures that favor gambling.

An example of which are those that come from Asian backgrounds and cultures. They will be more likely to gamble and develop gambling habits. Another study points out that cultural perceptions may be related to psychiatric disorders [click here].

That means it will be beneficial for therapists to learn about a patient's cultural background. This will help to provide a more efficacious mode of treatment that is custom tailored for each patient.

Taking this approach helps to build trust between clinician and patient. It also demonstrates openness since the therapist acknowledges the client's cultural background and belief system. Through this process cultural barriers are broken down and the treatment method can be adapted to the patient's unique profile accordingly.

CBT and Internet Addiction

The Center for Internet Addiction was established back in the year 1995. You can find their website at www.netaddiction.com. They provide support, information, as well as treatment options for people dealing with internet addiction.

Their clients can seek help through traditional and other forms of psychotherapy. However, they also rely heavily on a form of Cognitive Behavioral Therapy that is designed to address the unique facets of internet addiction. This type of CBT is called CBT-IA.

This type CBT has been shown to be quite effective as a mode of treatment or as a part of an overall treatment plan. One study suggests that patients were able to demonstrate improvements by the 8th session. That means they were better able to manage the symptoms of their addiction at that stage [click here to see an example]. Studies also show sustained improvement among patients during a follow up conducted six months after the conclusion of therapy sessions.

In another study [click here] results show that 95% of patients who underwent CBT-IA were able to manage their urges and addictions after 12 weeks of treatment. This mode of CBT also has greater sustainability since 78% of those treated were able to avoid any relapse 6 months after the conclusion of the series of therapy sessions.

Treatment of Choice

CBT-IA is today's treatment of choice for dealing with internet addiction. Note that a therapist will also use other tools in order to provide a full and comprehensive treatment for a patient.

For example, your therapist may use Young's Internet

Addiction Test (YIAT). YIAT is a tool that was developed using DSM-IV or Diagnostic and Statistical Manual IV, which is a standard for all psychiatric care.

CBT-IA uses the same criteria for pathological gambling and substance abuse. Of course the parameters have been modified for the specific type of addiction that is being addressed. For example, the 8-item scale used for substance abuse/problem gambling has been modified in CBT-IA.

The criteria used in CBT-IA include the following:

- Deception
- Mood modification
- Escapism
- Negative consequences
- Cognitive salience
- Behavioral salience
- Alternative recreational activities
- Relationship activities
- Neglecting everyday life
- Loss of control

These criteria are used to diagnose a patient. The system also uses a 5 point scale in the questionnaire. This helps to categorize the levels of internet use a patient may have.

Note that CBT-IA is a model that is uniquely designed for the treatment of internet addiction. It also applies Harm Reduction Therapy in the treatment process. This type of CBT or treatment model has three phases:

1. *Phase 1* – A therapist will use behavior modification to help a patient reduce the amount of time he or she spends on the internet. Sometimes there is more to it than to just reduce the total amount of time spent on the internet.

   At times a therapist will help a client to limit internet usage to more productive uses and not for questionable applications. An example of this is when a client uses the internet excessively to watch online porn. The goal is to help the patient abstain from spending time on online porn sites but still be able to use the internet for more productive purposes like school or work.

   One of the primary aims in this stage is to help clients with time management. As one study pointed out [click here], internet addicts feel a sense of displacement whenever they are online. In effect they neglect personal, social, and other aspects of their lives. This affects their work, studies, community, and other normal routines and relationships.

   However, it is important to remember that the main goal in this phase is to modify any unhealthy use of the internet. One of the tools that a therapist will use is called an internet activity diary. It will help evaluate a patient's behavior and the information gathered there can be used to devise a treatment plan later on.

   A huge part of the success in this phase however includes self-regulation. The patient must agree to have old patterns of addictive behavior to be interrupted. That means computer breaks should be removed, using alarms, using other activities to make better use of their time, block access to some sites, and remove bookmarks of some questionable internet resources.

2. *Phase 2* – Your therapist will then implement cognitive restructuring therapy to help deal with the denial that is often present in internet addicted people. This type of therapy is an effective tool to deal with the rationalizations that they may have to justify their excessive use of the internet.

   This is the treatment phase in CBT-IA and a variety of methods can be used. Phase 1 is more concerned with planning and data gathering. Phase 2 on the other hand is more concerned about the actual implementation of the ground rules that have been set between patient and clinician in Phase 1.

   In this stage maladaptive cognitions will be classified along with the associated triggers for each thought, memory, and feeling. For example, internet gaming addicts may believe that the offline world is something that is insignificant or undesirable.

   This can be due to the fact that in real life they have forsaken or abandoned their goals whereas when compared to the gaming world they have goals that they can accomplish time and again. This can lead to a psychological dependence in that in their online world they can enhance their self-esteem and gain renown and respect from their peers.

Cognitive restructuring is used by a therapist to break this line of reasoning. It challenges the belief and helps to rewire the patient's thought patterns. It helps the internet addict to reevaluate the rationality of their thoughts. Eventually they learn how to challenge the validity of their thoughts on their own without the assistance of a trained clinician.

3. *Phase 3* – The third phase of treatment involves the use of Harm Reduction Therapy. HRT can help identify other possible issues that are already coexisting with the patient's internet addiction and those that lead to a compulsive use of the internet. HRT helps patients to focus on their strengths and their unique capacity for change. It helps to empower them so that they can deal with feelings like low self-esteem minus any use of the internet.

CBT-IA can be used for in-patient and outpatient settings. There are other tools that a therapist might use such as the following:

- Internet Addiction Diagnostic Questionnaire (IADQ)
- Chen's Internet Addiction Scale (CIAS)

CBT as a Treatment for Eating Disorders

According to the UK National Institute for Health and Clinical Excellence (NICE), Cognitive Behavioral Therapy is the leading treatment for eating disorders, particularly for bulimia and anorexia. However, experts do not view CBT as a cure all and neither do they recommend it as such. Nevertheless, it is still highly recommended as a primary treatment option or as part of an overall treatment approach. It is also recommended by other institutes and centers such as the Center for Eating Disorders (www.eatingdisorder.org).

Take note that CBT, just like other treatment options for eating disorders, still need to work out and fine tune their treatment regimens. It should be pointed out here that the current type of CBT in use today is a modified improved second version of the original CBT approach for eating disorders.

Why was a change instituted in this practice? You see the first version of CBT for eating disorders (i.e. CBT-BN) produced only minimal successful results. Results from the original CBT show that only less than half of all the patients who actually completed their treatments have made any full and lasting recovery post treatment.

This is of course one of the shortcomings of CBT as a whole and another reason for critics of this practice to call for changes and improvements to be implemented [click here for an example]. The newer version of CBT for eating disorders, also known as CBT-E, is showing better results and looks like this modified version is a lot more effective than the original.

According to one study on anorexia nervosa, the largest one to date, CBT-E is an effective option for treating outpatients with this type of eating disorder. Reports show that 60% of these patients have reported good outcomes regarding their therapy. Another important key indicator here is that the relapse rate for patients is also quite low.

Still in the Works

Even though CBT has had some improvements for the treatment of anorexia, the results there can't be translated to other forms of eating disorders. Again, CBT is not a panacea, which means the treatment methodology that you used for one specific condition cannot necessarily be applied to another expecting similar success rates.

A good example of this is in the case for the treatment of binge eating. There is a type of CBT that was developed to address this eating disorder called CBT-BED. Yes, CBT-BED was able to produce marked effects on patients with this disorder. However, the question is that if it was truly effective then why is it that patients are still struggling with their weight gain.

CBT-E, just like other forms of CBT also has several treatment stages, which are the following:

1. Stage 1 – this is the initial or preparatory stage where the therapist and patient agree on the necessary treatment and changes that need to be done. As you can see, this stage is collaborative in nature, which is a standard in CBT practice. Real time self-monitoring is also established in this stage as well as weekly weigh ins, establishing regular eating patterns, and soliciting support from the patient's significant others.

2. Stage 2 – this stage is a transitional stage comprising of 2 meetings with a clinician. The meetings are usually set about a week apart. The progress that the patient has achieved is reviewed. The process, tools, and techniques either will be reinforced or revised.

3. Stage 3 – this is actually the main treatment phase. There will be 8 weekly appointments during this stage. The client's shape and weight will be addressed and evaluated during this stage along with rules on the patient's diet, event related eating changes, interpersonal problems, low self-esteem, and perfectionism.

4. Stage 4 – this is the final stage and it focuses on ending the treatment on a good note. There will usually be 3 appointments with a therapist in this stage and they will be set 2 weeks apart. Self-monitoring will be discontinued on this stage and the patient will continue weighing personally at home.

CBT Limitations

Remember that CBT is not a cure all and it is not to be expected to be a success in every case. For instance, medical reviews found out that CBT may not be an effective tool to help manage difficult behaviors in children who are raised in foster homes. It is also not helpful when used in conjunction with the treatment of tinnitus, but it can help reduce the levels of anxiety that is experienced by people with this medical condition.

Chapter 4: Methods of Access

Most of the time what people imagine about psychotherapy is where a patient sits on a comfortable couch in a psychiatrist's office—well, sometimes you lie down on the couch which is also perfectly fine. The patient then talks about his problems while the psychiatrist listens and asks questions. It is a guided conversation and notes will be taken along the way so as to track the client's progress.

Is that the same way with Cognitive Behavioral Therapy? Yes and more—you can actually choose the delivery method or method of access that works for you. One of the best ways to get CBT is with the help of a trained psychotherapist.

There is no question about that. However, sometimes it may be difficult to find a cognitive behavior based psychiatrist. For some access to one will mean traveling quite a distance and that just won't do since they have a lot of other things that they need to get done.

The good news is that CBT offers more than just the traditional mode of psychotherapy. You can get it through computer and internet based services, through an app on your phone, group sessions, and also by reading self-help manuals and workbooks.

So, which method of access is better?

Well, that depends on several factors. Someone with a really serious condition may require the direct supervision and care of a mental health worker or maybe a specialist. However, in the case of people who have problems that aren't in the same level may benefit from reading self-help books and/or computer and internet delivered CBT.

Note that some conditions will require the guide of a trained professional. For instance, a person with OCD undergoing exposure and response prevention will need someone to facilitate the experience. It cannot be done using a phone app, on a computer, or any self-help resource.

However, if you just want to test the waters and see if CBT is going to benefit you with your condition then maybe a phone app delivered form of CBT will be a cheaper and more convenient option. It all depends on your current state of affairs.

A Variety of Delivery Methods

Remember that CBT is usually a kind of treatment that is short-term. That means you shouldn't expect the treatment to go on for a very long time. A common treatment plan will involve around 12 sessions with each session lasting only about an hour long.

These sessions aren't conducted on a daily basis—you actually attend a weekly session. But your therapist will give you some homework to accomplish before the next scheduled appointment.

The scheduled sessions will be spread across 12 weeks or less.

Take note that there are CBT programs that are much shorter. For instance, you may find some centers offering treatment programs that only have an initial 4 sessions. If after the conclusion of the initial CBT sessions that you find you need more help then you will be given the opportunity to attend more CBT sessions after.

Note that there are CBT programs that tend to take longer. For instance, some programs will have 6 to 18 sessions. This means that it is a lot longer. Each meeting will still be around one hour each. However, you won't be meeting once a week. There will be a gap of 1 to 3 weeks in between each meeting. Every CBT program is different so it will be better to check with a clinic or provider and get the schedule directly from a CBT trained therapist.

Note that the delivery method in a therapy program may not always be the traditional face-to-face meeting with a therapist. Some of your sessions may include the following:

- **Group Sessions:** you will attend group activities with a facilitator. The group will be comprised of people who have similar problems. It is not exactly the same experience as you would get from group meetings such as Alcoholics Anonymous since there is plenty of structure in group sessions and your therapist will be following a treatment or training program.

- **Individual Sessions:** these are the one on one session with a therapist. Now some sessions will be conducted face to face however CBT practitioners today take advantage of modern technology. That is why some individual sessions can be done over the phone, through chat sessions, and also through video calls.

- **Computer Delivered or Phone App Delivered:** computer delivered CBT is usually conducted online. This method of delivery is also known as ICBT. There have been several studies (click here to see one) gives merit to the efficacy of computer delivered CBT. However, note that one shouldn't make ICBT their only source of therapy—but if it is the only one that you have access to at the moment then that is totally better than having nothing at all.

- **CBT through Self-Help Books:** your therapist will give you worksheets, workbooks, and other materials with tasks that you should complete on your own. These are self-help books that support the other sessions that you will be participating in. Remember that CBT sessions are usually held only once a week. You need something to reinforce the ideas and training that you have received.

Another source of CBT is separate third-party self-help books, such as this one. Should you rely on them as a sole source of treatment? That will depend on the level of anxiety or depression that you may be facing. CBT is also used by people who are looking for performance enhancement and other benefits and not just for the treatment of any condition. Self-help books may be a more practical option for these folks. Just remember that these books are just as effective as ICBT or phone based apps since there is no trained professional who can guide you along the way.

Structure of CBT Sessions

Here's what you can expect when you attend a typical CBT session. They may include the following:

- When the session starts your therapist will help you explore the details of the problem that you want to work with. This initial stage can be done individually or in groups. If you are attending a group session then your therapist may use tools like a worksheet to help you through the necessary steps.

- Some people may be struggling with more than one issue but you and your therapist must agree on which problems you will be focusing on during the sessions. You can only deal with so much and the sessions cannot address every single problem. You can always attend more therapy sessions later to deal with the other problems that have not been addressed during therapy.

- You will be working through exercises with your therapist during the scheduled meetings. These exercises are designed to help you explore your behaviors, feelings, and thoughts. Some of the exercises will involve the use of worksheets, sometimes videos may be used, at times you will be required to analyze and understand diagrams in order to learn new concepts and open your mind to other points of view or ways of thinking.

- There is usually no rush in CBT. The homework that will be given to you aren't rush projects. You do them and complete them on your own time. If you fail to complete a worksheet by the next session your therapist will help you with the details and you may continue working on it until the next meeting. You and your therapist will agree on the exercises and homework that you will tackle afterwards.

- Every succeeding session will usually begin with an appraisal of the previous session. You and your therapist will

Why Choose a Face to Face Therapy with a Specialist

Face to face sessions between you and a therapist is the typical method of access in Cognitive Behavioral Therapy. However, CBT with a therapist is usually the initial program that you will be introduced to. It is highly recommended that you start with that especially if this is your first time to try Cognitive Behavioral Therapy.

After face to face therapy sessions, other modes of access may be explored. There are studies that show that other methods of access apart from in person cognitive behavioral therapy sessions have the same beneficial effects. According to one report published by the Journal of the American Medical Association (JAMA), patients who receive CBT via telephone administration (i.e. T-CBT) is just as effective and at times is much better than face to face therapy.

In the short term, T-CBT had lower rates of attrition—that means there were fewer people who quit CBT treatment— compared to those who had treatment with an actual CBT practicing psychiatrist. That means telephone based or over the phone therapy was just as effective.

By the end of the treatment phases, it would appear that whether a patient went through in person or over the phone CBT they received the same benefits, which therefore means that you can augment treatment via over the phone correspondence between therapist and patient [click here to see the details of the report].

Long Term Advantage

So, if telephone based CBT produces the same effect as in person therapy sessions, why should you at least begin your cognitive based behavior therapy with an actual psychiatrist? The big difference is in the long term effects.

According to that June 6, 2012 JAMA report, 6 months after the conclusion of the therapy sessions, it was found that those who underwent in person therapy sessions were less depressed than those who only received it over the phone. On top of that those who had CBT face to face with a therapist were more likely to continue their treatment in the long term.

Why is Face to Face CBT Therapy Better?

According to another study [click here for details], there may be two important reasons why a face to face appointment may help you overcome stress, depression, and other issues in the long term.

The two cited possible reasons are as follow:

- Behavioral Activation
- Human Contact

The act of pushing or forcing yourself to go to the psychiatrist's clinic serves as a form of behavioral activation. That means you are helping yourself to get things started. You get a figurative push in the right direction by making you do something or try a new behavior that helps you resolve your own issues.

It is believed or posited that the very act itself of going to the clinic and attending the meeting physically is already therapeutic. This contributes to the maintenance of any gains that can be obtained from CBT sessions. New habits are formed and old constraining behavioral and cognitive barriers are being broken in the process.

The other reason is human contact. This one is slightly sketchy but it is definitely theorized. First off, the actual physical presence of a therapist in itself has no direct impact on how effective the CBT treatment will have.

However, it is believed that the presence of a therapist, maybe as an authority figure or something, has an impact in the treatment that it can help the patient maintain and retain whatever benefits that they may have received during session especially after any contact with the therapist has ceased.

But the actual effect of that clinician-patient interaction will still have to be verified. You see there are verbal and non-verbal channels that can still help maintain that contact and eventually establish and maintain that relationship of trust between both parties.

Don't Count Out Distance Therapy Just Yet

As it has been pointed out, other forms of communication and contact is still beneficial. They can be used to reinforce to the client what has been learned. You can add the fact that for patients who come in for treatment due to depression is more likely to respond and get better through CBT administered via telephone or any other form of long distance communication or media.

Telephone administration of CBT can help to lower attrition rates when it is combined with face to face appointments with a clinician. It helps overcome access barriers. This type of long distance communication is a big help to patients who live in remote places especially if they can't afford to travel long distances just to meet with a therapist.

This is also true for people who are recovering or are currently suffering from a serious health condition. Again, you can't expect these people to travel—not in the current state of their health. And of course we can't expect the psychotherapist to travel long distances since that will also leave the rest of his or her other patients without a primary care giver.

BIG TIP: according to the same study cited earlier, if you want to combine both face to face therapy and other modes of access then you should at least attend at least 5 or more initial face to face CBT treatment. It has been observed that patients who have had at least that many contacts with their therapist helps them overcome their own barriers to access primary service and they become more motivated to continue with their treatment.

Remember that the patient is very much involved in CBT. There is what is called a therapeutic alliance between caregiver and patient. The CBT therapist can help out if an assignment or exercise is too difficult for the patient.

Let's say a patient who is experiencing anxiety is having trouble talking to complete strangers. They can try out that exercise—the patient with the guidance of the therapist— but if it still is too difficult, the therapist can help by giving an easier exercise.

In this case they can both agree to have the patient talk to someone in the office that they have at least greeted once or twice but not really had an actual conversation. At least the person is no longer a complete stranger—just an acquaintance this time. They can even agree on who it is the client should talk to.

CBT and ICBT

ICBT, as it was explained earlier refers to CBT therapy sessions that are conducted with the help of computer technology. This method of access usually requires the use of a computer or even via an app on your phone. And on top of that you will usually require an internet connection so that the CBT app or computer applet can access an entire suite of resources to help you.

Simply put, ICBT is CBT that is delivered via the internet. It is a computerized version of this type of therapeutic intervention. It is also known or referred to by other names such as eCBT, CCBT, online CBT, and others. Note that ICBT is usually the name you call any CBT treatment or program that is delivered via the internet through an app or computer program. It is also sometimes spelled as iCBT, but of course it also refers to the same thing.

That means video calls do not belong to this category. There has to be a human component (the patient) and a non-human component (the app or website or computer program) in the process for the system to be called ICBT.

The Difference between CBT and ICBT

Let's go over the differences between CBT and ICBT. Later on we will go over the pros and cons of each option. Let's begin with a description of these two methods of access.

Observable Characteristics of Traditional CBT

- 4 to 20 sessions on average
- Usually done face to face with a trained clinician
- There is a potential for long wait times (it's sometimes hard to find an available CBT trained psychiatrist)
- Sometimes you may be required to secure a referral first or a recommendation
- There may not be a center, clinic, or therapist near your location that offers CBT
- There is a requirement for ongoing clinical support
- The out of pocket cost can be considerable
- The quality of the service varies from one therapist to the other

Observable Characteristics of ICBT

- Delivery is online
- Access to CBT training, material, and treatment is immediate (it all depends on the quality of your internet connection)
- It can be easily prescribed
- It is available to anyone who has an internet connection

- This is more of a self-motivated therapy (this can actually be both a pro and a con actually)
- It allows for an optional clinical support (i.e. a psychiatrist may be on standby to provide you with direct assistance)
- Fixed cost—and it is much more affordable compared to traditional CBT
- The quality of the service is consistent since everyone will be getting the same product/service (again this is both a pro and a con—it's a con because what if you need some specialized form of help? You won't get it because the service is uniform for all clients)
- The online CBT programs are usually shorter anywhere from 4 to 10 sessions only

What to Expect from ICBT Sessions

Here are some of the facets that you may observe out of ICBT sessions. Note that apps and online programs may be different. Some may have some of the features listed below and some may have fewer. You may also find ICBT products that have other features not listed below.

- *Online Questionnaires*

Your answers to these questions are vital and they will help the ICBT system to determine which course of treatment best suits you. In some systems your answers will be relayed to an actual psychiatrist for professional evaluation. That means in some apps and systems, your evaluation may take some time to get processed.

- *Cloud Based Schedules and Calendar*

Your data is stored in the cloud. That means you can access your information any time. You can access it through your phone or through your computer. The security is also pretty tight so you don't have to worry too much about your medical records and history during these sessions to get leaked out.
You can check your next scheduled meeting or session without any fuss. You can also review the information from your previous sessions as well as the homework that you need to accomplish.

- *Homework*

Just like in classic CBT you will also be given tasks to work on. You can get the instructions for the activities for the activities that you have to accomplish straight into your computer or phone. You can even setup reminders. Lesson summaries will also be provided to help reinforce what you have learned in the previous therapy session.

- *Multimedia and a Variety of Instructional Materials*

Visual learners and other folks can also take advantage of multimedia lessons, interactive lessons, video, and other lesson formats. You'll learn coping skills through a variety of teaching and learning methods.

- *Recovery Stories and Support*

Some ICBT programs have community based support where you can interact online with other people who have also subscribed to the service. Clinicians also take part in the discussions and also help to enhance the community spirit. You also get to learn about recovery stories from other people which will encourage you to progress further in your treatment and onto your eventual recovery.

- *Extra Resources*

There are plenty of other extra resources in other apps as well. There will be plenty of lessons and other assignments that you can work on in between each session. Just like in regular CBT, you work on them on your own time.

ICBT Limitations

Internet delivered CBT as well as other types of psychotherapy has been proven by numerous studies to be effective. They also provide support to traditional face to face interventions. However, ICBT does have similar shortcomings like in long distance therapy (e.g. T-CBT).

You can apply evidence based psychotherapy or any other form of therapy online. They also help a lot when it comes to monitoring a patient's progress and overall safety. However, online diagnoses can still be faulty and that means they are not fully reliable.

That is why you will still need the aid of an actual cognitive behavioral based clinician. This is especially true for patients who have more complex conditions. There is just no way to fully automate a psychiatric diagnostic system.

An actual therapist right there before you can spot minor details that an app or computer program would miss. On top of that, a therapist can also customize certain features of the CBT training or treatment.

Self-Help CBT Books and Group Therapy

Self-help books are a plenty and that is also true for those who want to learn more about CBT. Now, it is one thing to learn about CBT and totally different to actually go through an actual CBT treatment program. There are studies that show that CBT books can have a positive effect on individuals suffering from anxiety, PTSD, stress, and other similar conditions.

However, self-help books on CBT can also go only so far. They too have the same downsides as the other forms of CBT delivery. That is other than face to face therapy sessions with a trained psychiatrist. You can pick up lessons that work for you and cherry pick along the way.

There are problems with this approach as pointed out above. One study showed that self-help CBT books only provided significant help when it is used with the guidance of a clinician or another trained medical professional.

Group CBT therapy or group CBT for short is also another method of access that has been made available to patients. It has been shown to be effective for the treatment of depression and other mental health conditions.

One study reported that a psychiatric outpatient clinic had good results after patient records were analyzed. 44% of all their patients showed significant improvement at post treatment of their depression. 30% of them actually recovered, that is immediately after treatment. During a follow up period the number of clients who recovered went up as high as 57%. The lower results during post treatment were probably due to the 17.5% dropout rate [click here to see report].

What this means is that group CBT is a viable option for routine care of people suffering from depression and other mental health disorders. However, there are still a lot of people who do not get significant benefits from group therapy. That means the traditional face to face or one on one CBT mode of therapy still has an edge over other methods of access despite its aforementioned drawbacks.

Chapter 5: Types of Cognitive Behavioral Therapy

In this chapter we will look at the different types of Cognitive Behavioral Therapy. Note that some of them are pure therapies while others are may just be training exercises that can be combined with other forms of therapy.

Note that the list of CBT types mentioned here is not complete or comprehensive. Remember that CBT is a fairly new mode of psychotherapy and it is still growing. Newer types and modes of this therapy are being formulated and we should expect to see more developments to come in the future.

Brief Cognitive Behavioral Therapy

BCBT or Brief Cognitive Behavioral Therapy is a type of CBT that is best suited for people who have a lot of time constraints. If a regular therapy session will seem too long for you then BCBT may be a pretty good option.

It was developed by David M. Rudd for soldiers on active duty overseas. The objective was to prevent suicides and reduce suicide rates among those serving in the military.

BCBT has distinctive elements that make it very useful for treating patients with suicidal tendencies. These elements include the following:

- Collaborative

- Structured
- Directive
- Short term

BCBT as a Treatment for Suicidality in the Military

Suicide related deaths among military personnel in the US exceed the number of deaths that are combat related. This is also the same trend seen in both those who are still active in the military and also among war veterans.

The distinct elements of BCBT make it ideal for military personnel active or otherwise. It allowed men and women in military service to understand, cope, and master skills that are essential for them in their peculiar way of life.

It is also seen as a useful tool for soldiers who will have to self-manage rather than attend intensive ongoing psychotherapy. It is used as an effective tool to address Axis I and Axis II disorders, which include PTSD and major depression.

The following are the common elements used its many treatment protocols:

1. Developing a suicidality model that is easy to understand
2. A huge focus on treatment compliance
3. Target skills that are identifiable
4. Patients taking responsibility for their treatment
5. Providing access to emergency and crisis services
6. Documenting the treatment strategy agreed upon by the therapist and the patient

1. BCBT Suicidality Model That is Easy to Understand

BCBT uses the following easy to understand theoretical suicidality model. It may be presented a bit differently depending on your needs and conditions:

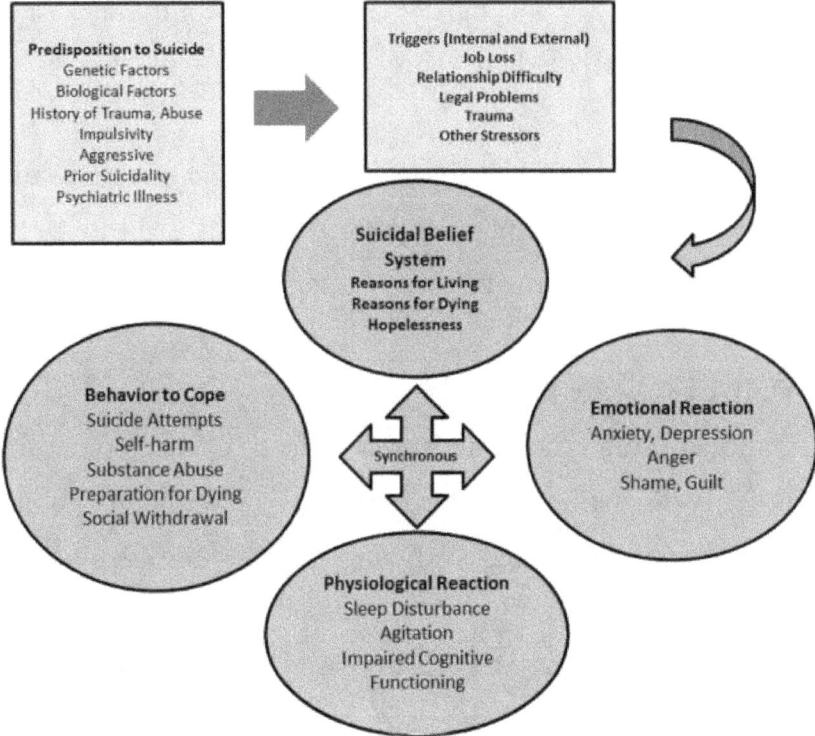

This model makes it easier for therapists to explain to patients why suicidal thoughts affect one's behavior and why some are thinking about killing themselves or have tried to kill themselves.

Note that these models will be constructed using a risk assessment interview. That means the models may be a bit different from one patient to another.

2. Treatment Compliance

Treatment compliance is a huge factor in CBCT. Remember that this type of CBT is short term and there won't always be a therapist to assist or provide service to a patient. That is why when a patient is not participating, non-compliant, or is performing poorly then the treatment will focus on compliance.

Treatment plans in BCBT will include clear and effective steps when there is non-compliance. Non-compliance is often seen as a reflection or outgrowth of the patient's inadequate skills.

3. Identifiable Skills

Patients will then be taught skills such as understanding cognitive distortions, interpersonal relationship skills, problem solving, anger management, and emotional regulation.

These skills are aimed at reducing suicidal thinking. Patients will also be given opportunities to practice these skills. BCBT places a huge focus on emotion regulation as well as on self-management.

4. Patients Taking Responsibility for Their Own Treatment

Since treatments won't be as frequent in BCBT, it is rational to place the treatment responsibility on the patient. Emphasis will be on self-control, self-awareness, and self-reliance.

Tools that will be used here include a Crisis Response Plan (CRP) and a Commitment to Treatment Agreement (CTA).

5. Availability of Emergency Services and Crisis Services

Plans will also be made to make both crisis and emergency services will be made readily available to the patient. The patient will also be trained to use these services appropriately and judiciously.

6. Treatment Plan Documentation

BCBT also places a huge emphasis on document both the treatment plan as well as the progress of patient. Tools that will be used for documenting purposes include journals, reasons for living cards, and others. Talk to your therapist regarding these tools.

BCBT Treatment Phases

There are three treatment phases in BCBT and each phase encompasses certain treatment strategies.

Treatment Phase	Tools/Strategies Involved
Phase 1 – Orientation	Means Restriction Crisis Response Commitment to Treatment Suicidality Model

	Reasons for Living Card Survival Kit Treatment Journal Lessons Learned
Phase 2 – Skill Focus	Worksheets for Skill Development Demonstrations Coping Cards Skill Refinement Practice
Phase 3 – Relapse Prevention	Skill Generalization Skill Maintenance

Phase one is the most detailed phase since it is supposed to be somewhat an immersive experience. Elements of this phase include:

- Treatment responsibilities will be outlined
- Safety plans and crisis responses will be formulated
- Commitments will be made
- Goals will be itemized
- Behaviors will be demonstrated and practiced

- Agreements will be signed

Phases two and three will have techniques and tools that are to be facilitated more by the clinician. It should be noted here that BCBT isn't only applicable to military personnel or to those who have suicidal tendencies. It has applications to other cases as well which includes people who experience anxiety, depression, and also those who may have a history of substance abuse.

Cognitive Emotional Behavioral Therapy

Cognitive Emotional Behavioral Therapy (CEBT) is a form of CBT that was developed to help people with eating disorders. Just like with BCBT it has been expanded so that it can also be applied to people who also experience other conditions such as anger issues, post-traumatic stress disorder (PTSD), people who experienced trauma, obsessive compulsive disorder (OCD), depression, and anxiety.

CEBT is used today as a type of pre-treatment. Its goal is to help prepare individuals and equip them with skills that will help them through long-term therapy. It is relatively new and it is specifically developed in order to help individuals who have problems expressing and experiencing their emotions.

Digging in a little bit deeper, CEBT is more of an extended form of Cognitive Behavioral Therapy. The treatment helps individuals learn how to evaluate the emotional basis of their anxieties and other distress.

After developing such an understanding, a person can then depend less on the coping behaviors that they have adopted (e.g. substance abuse, binge eating, etc.). CEBT can help you better understand the emotions that you experience as well as the way you express them. It works by challenging your present beliefs so that you can respond to any emotion adaptively.

The following is the model for CEBT as it is used for the treatment of eating disorders:

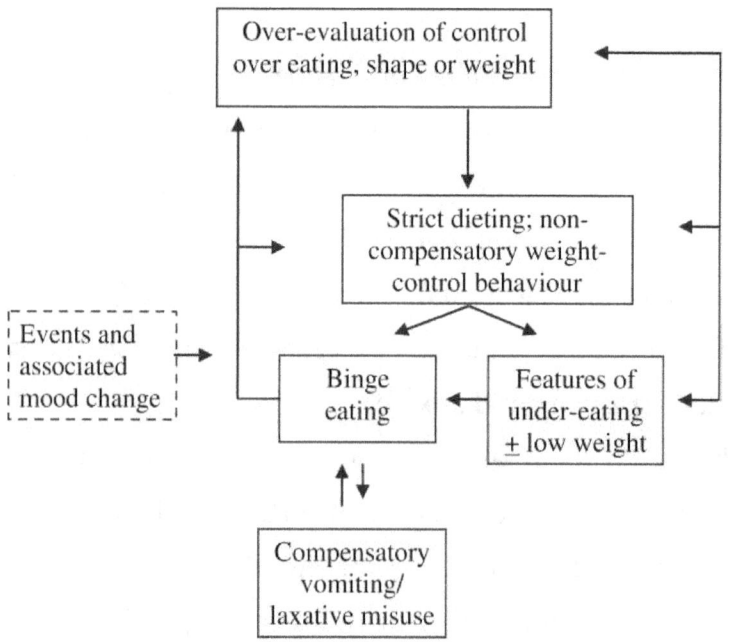

Who is CEBT For?

CEBT is not only for people who binge eat or have any other

form of eating disorder. It is also for trauma victims, people with low self-esteem, and also anger problems. Cognitive Emotional Behavioral Therapy was developed by Dr. Emma Gray Corstorphine. It has since been expanded upon to help people having trouble experiencing different types of emotions.

Note that even though CEBT can resolve binge eating for you (for instance), it will not be a solution to being overweight. It can only help with one aspect of a weight loss regimen. It can't be used as the lone formula for losing weight.

How Does CEBT Work?

Cognitive Emotional Behavioral Therapy combines Dialectical Behavioral Therapy (DBT), Cognitive Behavioral Therapy (CBT), Acceptance and Commitment Therapy (ACT), Mindfulness meditation, and experiential exercises.

It is used as a preparatory treatment so that people can handle their emotions better. With the exercises that you will undergo, you will be prepared to face the often times emotionally charged therapy sessions.

The elements of mindfulness training help to add a different dimension to this form of CBT. It paves the way for self exploration as well as creativity when exploring one's inner reasons and cognitions.

It helps people who struggle with anxiety, depression, harsh self-criticism, extreme control, and perfectionism. You can say that it is also a gentle approach and it can be used as a lifelong practice.

Patients benefit greatly by learning to accept their emotions as well as their feelings. It also helps you understand that your thoughts and feelings are not necessarily the reality behind things or circumstances or events.

When you learn to accept them and allow emotions to come and go real healing then begins. You also learn how not to be overwhelmed by these feelings. It allows you to be calm all throughout the surge or emotions that you will go through in life.

CEBT teaches you to be calm and observant giving you back the necessary control even through very emotional situations. Emotions whether they are pleasant or unpleasant will come and go.

However, the training that you will receive will teach you not to be attached to those feelings. But note that you will also not push them away. Feelings will be acknowledged and then you will learn the nature of such feelings. You will learn that your feelings may be a part of you but they do not define who you are.

Structured Cognitive Behavioral Training

Structured Cognitive Behavioral Training (SCBT) is also

known as CBTraining or Cognitive Behavioral Training. Note the name—this is not actually a form of therapy per se but is more of a systematic training approach that uses the principles and core concepts of Cognitive Behavioral Therapy.

You can say that this is CBT that has been repurposed for training individuals whether they have issues to contend with or not. SCBT has the following major characteristics:

- It is regimented
- It is systematic
- Most of it takes on a workshop approach

The goal behind the training that you will receive in SCBT is to enable you to replace any kind of emotion dependent and/or dysfunctional behavior. CBTraining also assumes that human behavior is deeply rooted in emotions, thoughts, and beliefs.

Today, CBTraining is used in the fields of criminal psychology as well as in behavioral health. Practitioners also make use of methodologies from behavioral change theories in tandem with CBT models and methods.

What Makes SCBT Different?

Both CBT and SCBT have the same philosophy and that is thoughts and feelings are inextricably linked. However, SCBT assumes that whenever we are in an emotionally dependent relationship we make our decisions based on our emotions. That means we lose the ability to make rational choices when our emotions take precedence.

Training

As stated earlier, one key difference between CBT and SCBT is that the former is a type of therapy and the latter is more like training than therapy. When CBT has been transformed into a type of training program a set schedule will be put into place.

That also means there is a determined time when training begins and also a time when training will be terminated. The training will also be broken down into progressive phases. Each phase will have a particular point of focus.

Goal

Participating in such a training course will help to retrain your brain. The overall goal is to help you get rid of thinking patterns that are emotionally dependent or emotionally driven.

Classes

Another difference is that if you undergo SCBT, you will be attending classes—or something similar to that. You will be quizzed about the things that you learned from training. You will also have to complete homework, which is why they are called classes.

Writing Therapy

Much of the work that you will be doing in SCBT will be based on writing therapy. Expect to do a good deal of journaling work and other recollection activities. You will be jotting down the details of your emotional experiences.

It has been found that the trauma and stress of an individual can greatly be reduced when they get to express their emotions in writing.

Structured According to Specific Dependencies

In therapy the focus is on the individual and his or her own experiences. That is why CBT can be custom tailored to the needs of individual patients. But that is not the case with SCBT.

The focus in SCBT is in changing the dependency of the individual. That is to be addressed in the exercises, classes, and homework. The idea is to create rapid change in training participants. There will be individual work and also group work (if you are participating in a group class).

In the case of children who participate in such training programs, they will undergo social behavioral modification. The idea of this educational approach is to implant new life skills in participants and make those skills a permanent part of their way of thinking. They will eventually learn that there is an alternative to an emotionally based response and how to use it as needed.

Urge Conditioning and Desensitization

Apart from other kinds of therapy CBTraining or SCBT can also be used to help people with addictions and other similar types of destructive behavior. In contrast to other treatment approaches which are based on urge avoidance, SCBT emphasizes urge conditioning and desensitization.

These techniques were first used on people with gambling addictions and were found to be quite effective. The approach is like this. We usually would think along the lines of an out of sight-out of mind approach.

SCBT training programs will do the opposite. A gambling addict will be shown and brought to environments that remind the person of his or her addiction. Participants will be exposed to the triggers that bring about their urges.

Eventually their training will involve regaining control. Sure they will feel the urge to gamble but participants will also slowly learn to be comfortable with these urges. After a certain amount of practice they will be desensitized to these urges.

They will realize that there is a gap between the urge and the act—a moment when they can choose to either give in to the urge or just let it pass by. Since SCBT is a training process, the urges that participants feel will methodically be stripped of their appeal and influence. Participants will learn to acknowledge and use their power to choose.

Performance Enhancement

SCBT can also be applied to different fields other than being part of a therapeutic modality to address different emotional and mental conditions. It can also be used to help improve the performance of people who may not exactly be suffering from any form of malady.

For instance, one study from West Virginia University focused on using SCBT to help college basketball players improve their free throw performance. In their study, the test subjects were videotaped to help measure any cognitive changes that may have happened.

The study suggests that SCBT can help improve an athlete's performance in the basketball court. They found that study participants improved 50%, 78%, and 88% of the time during the course of the training.

However, it should be noted here that results were mixed both for cognitive changes as well as playing performance. However, the results were generally positive with improvements showing up on the test subjects' scores.

Participants in this study were taught deep relaxation techniques, coping strategies, as well as mental rehearsals before an actual game. The training helped players to manage the amount of stress that they experience during a game and improve their free throw shooting overall.

Now, if SCBT can help improve the sport performance of athletes then there is a possibility that such cognitive training programs can help other people improve their performances in other areas.

Another study involved job hunters who were having problems during interviews. They too also experienced improved performance during interviews. They didn't get hired a lot faster but they became more confident when facing an interviewer and they performed much better during any Q&A

session.

Moral Reconation Therapy

Moral Reconation Therapy or MRT for short is a type of Cognitive Behavioral Therapy that is used for felons and convicts to help them overcome Anti-Social Personality Disorder or ASPD.

This type of behavioral therapy can also be used to help people who are trying to recover from substance abuse. It helps them reduce the likelihood of returning to their former habits and lifestyles.

This treatment approach is systematic which is a bit similar to the approach in Structured Cognitive Behavioral Training. Of course, there are differences between the two. MRT is a form of therapy after all and not just a training course that is based on CBT.

The goal in MRT is to prevent the patient from re-offending or going back to old destructive habits. The focus on MRT is to help the patient to increase his or her moral reasoning, which makes it unique compared to the other forms of CBT that have already been discussed. You can say that this takes on a rather moral approach compared to the rest.

The psychological models used in MRT addresses a person's behavioral, social, and moral growth. It also targets their egos as well. Studies have shown that this type of therapy can also help improve a person's moral reasoning of criminal offenders as well as those who are recovering from various addictions.

Another thing that makes MRT distinct from other forms of CBT is that it focuses more on group therapy. This is due to the fact that holding one on one therapy sessions with criminal offenders especially those suffering from ASPD may trigger narcissistic behavior.

However, that doesn't mean that one-on-one MRT sessions aren't possible. In cases where there is no worry of triggering narcissistic behavior (e.g. in the case of drug abuse patients and others) then one-on-one therapy sessions can be put into place. However group sessions will still be used as part of the overall training program. That is something that therapists will try to avoid at all cost since it does not contribute to the patient's well-being.

Just like other forms of CBT, moral reconation therapy also follows the same philosophy in that it is assumed that the factors that influence a person's behavior are his beliefs, thoughts, and attitudes. This is one of the treatment approaches that have been given the nod by the Substance Abuse and Mental Health Services Administration.

There are several treatment approaches that may be involved and it varies from one treatment provider to another. Here are some of the treatments that a provider or MRT therapist may apply:

- Development of frustration tolerance
- Hedonism reduction

- Developing higher stages of moral reasoning
- Self-concept enhancement
- Positive Identity Formation
- Current Relationship Assessment
- Positive habits and behavior reinforcement
- Attitudes, beliefs, and behavior confrontation

How Does Moral Reconation Therapy Work?

MRT is a type of treatment program that is best suited for patients who are rather resistant to other forms of psychotherapy. It can become the treatment option of choice where other modes of cognitive treatment are inappropriate in some way. You can also try this form of treatment if other forms of treatment have been tried and have failed.

When this form of treatment is used for substance abusers (or any condition where this MRT is applicable for that matter) the primary approach is to reinforce moral reasoning when they formulate judgments and decisions.

Patients are also taught to enhance their positive identities as well as enhancing their own self-image. MRT also helps training participants to move away from a hedonistic mindset where decisions are made purely from pain or pleasure. They are taught and trained to a method of thinking that takes into account a concern for the welfare of other people as well as the social rules that every person in society must abide by.

Note that there will be homework that training participants

will be expected to complete. Apart from that there are also structured group exercises that patients should participate in. The overall structure of MRT trainings may include any of the following:

- Coming face to face with one's beliefs, attitudes, and behaviors.
- Learning to assess one's current relationships
- Learning to reinforce healthy behaviors and habits
- The construction of a positive identity
- Building a healthy self-concept
- Reducing self-destructive tendencies

Who is MRT for?

Today, Moral Reconation Therapy is specifically aimed at helping certain members of society and not only inmates or people in correctional facilities. They may also fit a specific profile, which includes anyone who is within the ages of 18 to 55 years old, war veterans, trauma survivors, and male and female. You don't need to have any sort of criminal history so that MRT can apply to you.

A lot of MRT programs are self-paced and open ended. It can be used across different systems and it can be integrated with other therapies and trainings. It is culturally neutral and the language and attitudes subscribed in the programs are gender sensitive.

The programs also embrace a variety of learning styles.

However, the approach of many programs is more of an inside out process. Even though MRT providers and practitioners may vary in their specific approaches, there is still a standard curriculum that provides a kind of structure for facilitators.

A huge part of the training emphasizes feedback as well as plenty of client reflection. That means patients are given all the opportunities to identify their unique strengths. This kind of training environment enhances a participant's problem solving skills and it eventually leads one to learn self-direction and autonomy.

Six Stages of Moral Reasoning

MRT makes use of Kohlberg's 6 stages of moral reasoning which are as follows:

Level 1—Pre-Conventional Morality
Punishment and Obedience Stage (pleasure vs. pain)
Instrumental Relativist Stage (backscratching)
Level 2—Conventional Morality
Interpersonal Concordance Stage (approval seeking)
The Rules are the Rules, The Law is the Law Stage
Level 3—Post Conventional Morality
Social Contract Stage
Universal Ethical Principles Stage

A lot of training participants start at Level 1 or stage 1 and 2. The goal is to help clients move from level 1 to level 3 in the above outlined stages.

Sample Group Process

The following is a sample group process that may be applied in an MRT program. The one that you may participate in could be a bit different but it will have a lot of similar characteristics and training phases.

- There will be one facilitator and several co-facilitators involved.
- Groups or classes will be made up of 5 to 15 participants.
- Training sessions are conducted once or twice a week.
- Each session lasts from 1.5 to 2 hours.
- Exercises are given to participants and constitute a kind of homework. Participants are expected to complete these exercises before attending the next training session. The facilitators review and approve the work submitted by participants.
- MRT programs can have as many as 20 to 30 total sessions.
- A client is said to have completed the entire MRT training if he or she is able to pass up to the 12th step of training.
- Groups are usually open ended. That means

- participants are allowed to enter the program at any time and work on the exercises at their own pace.
- In MRT groups are continuously ongoing with some participants entering early or even late, which is totally fine. Participants are expected to complete the program sequentially from step 1. Group members enter and graduate as part of an ongoing group process, which makes the program dynamic.

Stress Inoculation Training

Stress Inoculation Training or SIT is a type of cognitive based training related to but is slightly different from Stress Inoculation Therapy, which is also abbreviated as SIT (the main focus of this section is on the training and not so much on the therapy). Both of these help people respond better to stress and prepare them to face stressful situations. So, what's the difference?

Stress Inoculation Therapy helps people deal with the current things that are already stressing them out. Stress Inoculation Training on the other hand prepares people and helps them to cope with stressful conditions that may and will occur in the future.

Why "Inoculate"?

The main idea behind SIT is in "inoculation." Think of it as a kind of flu shot. When you get inoculated for the flu virus your body introduced or injected with a weaker variant of the virus so that it can produce T-cells or natural defenses that can counteract the virus.

SIT works the same way. You are inoculated with small scale stressful situations so that you can create your own natural defenses against similar future stressful conditions or situations. In the case of inoculation therapy, you are getting equipped with the tools to help you cope with your current stressors.

Goals of SIT

Stress Inoculation Training is usually applied along with other training and therapy. The goal of course is to help a person gain stress coping skills and also broaden whatever skills that one may have already have.

Another goal is for the person to learn how to boost his or her confidence despite a stressful condition so that they may be able to apply whatever coping skills they have learned.

Participants in this training program are also taught how to adjust the skills that they have learned. You see, there is no such thing as a skill or coping mechanism that applies to all situations. It doesn't mean that you have learned how to cope with situation A that the skills you used there will also work for situation B. However, you can adjust your coping strategy so that the coping tools you have acquired can be used and be made suitable for other situations as well.

SIT Training Phases

Stress Inoculation Training has three phases. They include the following:

1. Initial Conceptualization
2. Skills Acquisition
3. Application and Follow Through

Initial Conceptualization: in this phase the therapist or the facilitator of the training will educate participants and patients about the nature of stress. Part of that training or education is the two elements of stress which our bodies will go through. These two things occur when we experience either anxiety or fear of a thing, person, or event.

The two elements are the following:

- *Heightened physiological arousal* – the signs of heightened physiological arousal include muscle tension, chills, that feeling of having a lump in your throat, increased heart rate, and sweating. You may have heard of the fight or flight response—that is pretty much what you experience as it is described here.

- *Visualization and expectations* – our thoughts will interpret every situation and we assess if we are in danger or not. For instance a lot of people will say that they are afraid of knives. However, we all own knives. So, the question is how come we are afraid of knives if we own one at home.

What really happens is that we interpret and appraise every situation. Along with that evaluation we also interpret our own physiological arousal with regard to fear. The combination of the interpretation of physical arousal and the appraisal of that possible danger creates the anxiety that we feel.

More often than not, people make stressful situations worse by due to their own bad coping habits. People do these habits rather unconsciously. A facilitator or therapist will help patients the patients to formulate a better understanding of the stressors that one is facing.

Another important point that should be learned by participants is the fact that stressors are different. They are that stressors are nothing more than creative opportunities and puzzles that you will have to solve. The paradigm and outlook shifts from obstacles to doable challenges.

Participants are also taught to use acceptance based coping so that they can deal with certain aspects of conditions that they cannot change at all. Active interventions on the other hand will be practiced for aspects of stressors that can be changed.

Skills Acquisition: in this phase of SIT the facilitator or therapist will help participants to select skills that are custom tailored to the current stressful situations that they are facing.

The skills will be selected depending on the vulnerabilities and strengths of patients/training participants.

They will be taught how to regulate their emotions, problem solving communication, cognitive appraisal, and socialization skills. All of the skills necessary for the patient's unique needs will be selected in this phase.

Facilitators will focus training in the following aspects:

- Communication skills
- Relaxation training
- Emotional self-regulation
- Cognitive restructuring

Application and Follow Through: in this phase the participants will be given a lot of opportunities to practice the coping skills and strategies that have been selected. A variety of simulation methods will be used.

The situations that will be simulated will be made as real as it can be. The following activities will be used in this stage: behavioral practice repetition, role playing stressful situations, coping routines, vicarious learning, modeling, and visualization exercises.

Stress Inoculation Training can be conducted in groups as well as in one-on-one sessions. The size of groups can vary. Training sessions and interventions can last anywhere from 20 minutes to 40 minutes.

Trainings and therapy sessions can be scheduled weekly or bi-weekly. Most of the time a participant will attend a total of 8 to

15 sessions. After the last session, participants will also attend a few follow up sessions that will be schedule anywhere within 3 to 12 months after the training course is completed.

Who is Stress Inoculation Training For?

SIT can benefit people who are suffering from the following conditions:

- Performance anxiety (e.g. public speaking, sports, dating)
- Stressful life situations (e.g. relocation, unemployment, divorce)
- Chronic mental illness
- Problems with anger management
- Depression due to trauma
- Anger issues related to trauma
- Pain related disorders
- PTSD
- Severe anxiety
- Specific phobias

SIT can also become a preventive option for people for people who may be suffering from different kinds of serious medical issues. Examples of which include first degree burns, rheumatoid arthritis, hypertension, and cancer. It can also be a beneficial option for people who are in the preparation stage before undergoing a major medical procedure.

SIT as a Treatment for PTSD

SIT is one of the go to therapies that therapists use today for treating and addressing issues with Post Traumatic Stress Disorder or PTSD. It has been found to be effective for people who use avoidance when they experience anxiety due to an event they have experienced in the past.

SIT is used in tandem with other types of therapy to help people overcome the fear they feel when recalling memories and familiar situations. Patients use this fear as a kind of preventive measure. For instance, a rape victim may prefer to avoid dating, getting into relationships, and going out with someone in public because he or she fears getting attacked again.

A lot of studies have shown the effectiveness of stress inoculation when it comes to working with patients with PTSD. One study that was conducted back in 2002 [click here] showed that patients who underwent a variety of training and therapy had better responses to stressors. Some of the participants underwent SIT, Eye Movement Desensitization and Reprocessing Stress Disorder (EMDR), and Prolonged Exposure training.

A form of SIT called PRESIT (Pre-Deployment Stress Inoculation Training) was used to train marine personnel before they were deployed to specific missions. The PRESIT training was designed to help the soldiers to cope with stressors related to combat and war.

PRESIT involved 3 steps:

1. Education regarding combat stress control
2. Training on coping skills that focuses on breathing techniques with the help of biofeedback.
3. Practicing the first two steps by being exposed to a stressor environment via video.

Studies show that the soldiers who underwent PRESIT were better able to cope with stressful combat situations.

SIT for Cancer Patients

There may be more than 200 known types of cancer but they have something in common – they all produce immense stress. As if the pain they cause is already too much, having to suffer stress and anxiety because of this disease adds insult to injury.

Stress inoculation has been used in many cases and studies to help patients reduce anxiety and stress in cancer patients [click here to see the medical report]. Studies show that there are no downsides to using SIT for cancer patients. It can help them with any preconditioned fears that they may have developed it helps to reduce unwanted yet related behaviors toward their fear like vomiting and others.

Mindfulness-Based Cognitive Behavioral Hypnotherapy

Mindfulness-Based Cognitive Behavioral Hypnotherapy (MCBH) is a kind of Cognitive Behavioral Therapy that combines mindfulness practices with hypnotherapy. It is more of an awareness approach to so that patients can address any tendencies that may get triggered depending on specific stimuli. Just like the other forms of CBT that have been discussed here, MCBH takes on a step by step approach.

You can think of it as a form of CBT with hypnotherapy. Of course hypnotherapy isn't a must in CBT however it can positively influence the entire cognitive process. You will still focus on the current problems that you need to deal with but this time hypnotherapy will help you enter a relaxed dreamlike state that makes things easier.

Hypnotherapy and mindfulness techniques magnify the effects of cognitive based methods. Your conscious thoughts are suspended allowing you

What is Hypnotherapy?

Most of us think of that swinging pendulum or the ever famous pocket watch on a chain when we talk about hypnosis and hypnotherapy. Of course that only happens in the movies—although you may see some people still do that. In the case of CBT + hypnotherapy or cognitive hypnotherapy modern neuroscience is put to use with the practice of hypnosis.

That means everything is scientifically based. It takes into the account that we all naturally enter into a state of hypnotic trance whether it is assisted or not. This natural state of mind is what is used in Mindfulness-Based Cognitive Behavioral Hypnotherapy.

In this scientific approach to hypnosis you will never be put under the control of someone else. You will never lose control of the situation because the goal is to bring you to a relaxed hypnotic state where your memories and past experiences can't get to you thus allowing you to better analyze and create more constructive thought patterns. In the end you will learn essential cognitive and mindfulness skills a lot faster.

What Can MCBH Be Used For?

As we have already discussed in this book, one of the conventional uses of CBT is for treating anxiety, depression, and other related disorders. We have also mentioned the fact that it can also be added to a lot of other treatment regimens including those that deal with physical health symptoms like skin conditions, pain, as well as IBS or irritable bowel syndrome.

MCBH is also very effective deep rooted emotional issues. If you feel that you have been suffering from deeply rooted issues or if your therapist has determined that these issues still haunt you today then you might want to try MCBH. It has been used for issues like relationship problems, bereavement, the fear of falling, anger management, panic attacks, and low self-esteem. MCBH is also currently being used to assist with overcoming lifestyle issues and unwanted habits such as teeth grinding and smoking. It uses the same CBT plus mindfulness plus hypnotherapy techniques and principles that are also applied and used for treating phobias.

This type of Cognitive Behavioral Therapy can also be used for other similar issues such as keeping a healthy weight. Some experts consider it as an alternative treatment to help with weight loss. It is also used as a method to help people with eating issues.

It isn't focused solely in the treatment of various physical, emotional, and mental conditions. It can also be applied to other areas of life such as the level of performance in one's professional life. It is used to help train businessmen and other professionals to achieve goals that they previously thought was out of their reach. It is used to help people from becoming comfortable with public speaking to improving their sales pitches.

What to Expect

MCBH can be done through individual or as a group therapy. Sessions can be on a weekly schedule with two hour sessions each. It can also be structured as an eight week program. More frequent sessions can also be scheduled as needed.

Therapy sessions of course will be led by a therapist. During the sessions you will be taught different meditation techniques along with the principles of cognition. There you will be taught the same rudiments taught in CBT such as the relationship between your thoughts and your feelings.

Your therapist may give you homework during the days outside of therapy sessions. This will allow you to practice mindful meditation on your own. You will also be given a lot of opportunities to practice breathing techniques and other relaxation methods.

Chapter 6: Criticisms

When talking about the criticisms laid down against CBT it should be remembered that the critiques are aimed at the entire new wave of treatments. It is not just referring to the traditional or classical form of CBT that was conceptualized decades ago.

A lot of the critiques often focus on that part of CBT where the drive is to alter negative self-concepts. That means the charge is usually more on the assumption of an irrational or negative self-beliefs rather than on behavior modification. However, there are critiques on behavior modification as well, although they are not as numerous as the ones for the cognitive assumptions and methodologies applied in CBT.

The competing view is that instead of the assumed negative cognitive beliefs that the patient already has, there are negative activating experiences that lead to such beliefs and/or behaviors. These activating experiences are believed to be the root cause of anxiety and depression.

However, both in CBT and psychoanalysis, it is believed that dysfunctional behavior has the same effects—it doesn't matter which view you take on it. It produces withdrawal from conventional human goals, the loss in investment in people, and a general sense of defeat.

Again, the alternative approach advocated by CBT is that one must restructure irrational or distorted beliefs and shift it to a more balanced and accurate beliefs (i.e. positive beliefs). Many studies have shown that CBT in many ways is superior to a medical approach when it comes to treating anxiety and depression.

However, it should be noted here that CBT is not without its downsides, which is also part and parcel of the criticisms against this therapeutic practice. We'll go over some of the more common critiques and downsides of CBT in this chapter.

Symptoms or Cognitive Causes

According to one critic it would appear that in the Cognitive Behavioral Therapy model, the symptoms of depression are confused with the cognitive causes. For example, one of the core symptoms of depression is a negative self-concept.

Examples of negative cognition include the following:

- Negative cognitive shift (i.e. all the negative aspects and views about oneself is either blocked out or filtered)
- Exaggeration of negative experiences
- Overgeneralization
- Selective abstraction
- Jumping to conclusions
- Dichotomous thinking (the all or nothing way of judging things)
- Wrong interpretation of events, personal interactions, and other experiences

- Unpleasant memories
- Negative predictions
- Self-criticism
- Self-blame
- Low-self esteem

For many people who suffer from depression, anxiety, and other related issues, these so-called negative cognitions take over the person's internal monologue or internal dialogue. They permeate a person's negative self-talk.

The question put out there is this—are the things in that list above really cognitive causes or are they really just the symptoms? In other words, the critique is that these are not really cognitive reasons but they are only symptoms of the core issue.

Accuracy of Negative Self-Assessment

Another critique leveled against CBT is the fact that a lot of the programs put a huge premium on negative self-assessment. Critics point to research that suggests that a person's positive self-evaluation can turn out to be more maladaptive and also dysfunctional.

Since CBT doesn't always look into such inaccuracies in a person's positive personal evaluation, it generally misses some important points about the individual. These critics point out that it is these positive self-assessments rather than the negative self-assessments that people make that are actually inaccurate and full of bias. This is according to data that was gathered in the workplace, education, and in health practice.

Relative Effectiveness

Another critique has to do with CBT's relative effectiveness. Now this is a big issue because the criticism doesn't only come from those who don't practice CBT in their psychiatric practice but there are CBT practitioners who also complain about its effectiveness as well.

There are studies that support the effectiveness of CBT. However, there are also studies that question its effectiveness. Some reviews and reanalysis of previous studies also render the positive and affirming results as questionable.

Just like other methods of psychotherapy, CBT is also prone to the fact that a lot of the clinical studies that support it are not double blind studies. Double blind studies should be conducted in a way that either the study participants and/or the therapists do not know if actual CBT is used or just a placebo (i.e. something that has no therapeutic effect).

In some studies it has been shown that CBT is just as good as any other treatment for schizophrenia and it also does not reduce any potential rates for relapse. There were very few studies on CBT as a treatment for major depressive disorder so they can't be used as a conclusive tool to gauge its efficacy. CBT has also been demonstrated in a few studies to be ineffective for the treatment of bipolar disorder relapse. Nevertheless, the debate is still on and there are those who question the way the reviews selected the research that should be reevaluated.

High Dropout Rates

A dropout is when a client decides to discontinue a treatment even if a clinician advises against it. Whenever such a thing happens, it usually raises a lot of questions. It is also seen as a possible failure of the procedure that was undertaken. There will always be an inquiry on the dropout rate of a therapeutic approach. Experts will also want to find out at what stage in a treatment are dropout incidents likely to occur. Another important thing that everyone wants to find out is the reasons for clients dropping out of a treatment procedure.

According to a 2015 study [click here] the dropout rate for CBT participants may go as high as 15.9% during the pretreatment stage. That is even before any actual CBT has been done for patients. That should be understandable since people can decide whether they want to begin treatment or not—this one is out of the hands of the therapist.

However, what is alarming is the higher incidence of dropouts during treatment. The rate goes up to 26.2%. That means more people tend to drop out of CBT treatment during the time they are going through the process.

The following are seen as factors associated with this

phenomenon

1. Number of sessions
2. Treatment setting
3. Format and delivery of the treatment
4. Problems with diagnosis

Even though CBT as a practice does have a high dropout rate, it should be pointed out that this is also happening in other forms of psychotherapy as well. In fact CBT also shares some of the same difficulties faced in medical practice in general.

Some experts suggest that operational definitions and other elements of CBT practice should be standardized in order to reduce the dropout rates. What we have today is a conglomeration of different types of CBT and yes there is no standard set for all of them.

Conclusion

I'd like to thank you and congratulate you for transiting my lines from start to finish.

I hope this book was able to help you to understand how CBT works, its strengths as well as its weaknesses. I also hope that by trying the exercises described here in this book you can decide if CBT is a viable treatment option for you.

If you find that Cognitive Behavioral Therapy is a good option then the next step is to find a clinician with background in CBT near you.

I wish you the best of luck!

Sources

https://www.tandfonline.com/doi/full/10.1080/08995605.2012.736325

https://www.ncbi.nlm.nih.gov/pmc/articles/PMC4041920/

http://dctraumacounseling.com/cognitive-emotional-behavior-therapy-cbet/

https://www.thebritishcbtcounsellingservice.com/therapy/cognitive-emotional-behavioural-therapy-2/

http://www.foresightguide.com/emotional-cognitive-behavioral-therapy-and-self-therapy

https://www.ncbi.nlm.nih.gov/pubmed/28430364

https://www.eatingdisorder.org/treatment-and-support/therapeutic-modalities/cognitive-behavioral-therapy/

https://www.ncbi.nlm.nih.gov/pubmed/20599136

https://www.ncbi.nlm.nih.gov/pmc/articles/PMC2928448/

http://self.gutenberg.org/articles/Cognitive_behavioral_therapy

https://link.springer.com/article/10.1007/BF01173095

https://positivepsychologyprogram.com/cbt-cognitive-behavioral-therapy-techniques-worksheets/

https://aforeverrecovery.com/our-programs/activity-group-therapy/moral-reconation-therapy/

https://www.pyramidhealthcarepa.com/moral-reconation-therapy/

https://whatworks.college.police.uk/toolkit/Pages/Intervention.aspx?InterventionID=26

https://www.ncbi.nlm.nih.gov/pmc/articles/PMC4743280/

https://www.ncbi.nlm.nih.gov/pmc/articles/PMC4462062/

https://www.mentalhelp.net/articles/stress-inoculation-therapy/

https://www.verywellmind.com/stress-inoculation-training-2797682

https://blog.cognifit.com/stress-inoculation/

https://www.ncbi.nlm.nih.gov/books/NBK64948/

https://www.ncbi.nlm.nih.gov/pmc/articles/PMC4041920/

https://www.apa.org/ptsd-guideline/patients-and-families/cognitive-behavioral

https://www.psychologytoday.com/us/basics/cognitive-behavioral-therapy

https://www.thrivetalk.com/3-phases-cognitive-behavioral-therapy-cbt/

https://www.helpguide.org/articles/stress/relaxation-techniques-for-stress-relief.htm/

http://suffolkcognitivetherapy.com/web/specialties/history-of-cbt/

https://beckinstitute.org/about-beck/our-history/history-of-cognitive-therapy/

https://www.sciencedirect.com/science/article/pii/S0924933817314761

https://www.foundationsrecoverynetwork.com/development-cognitive-behavioral-therapy/

https://www.mind.org.uk/information-support/drugs-and-treatments/cognitive-behavioural-therapy-cbt/cbt-sessions/#Types

https://www.sciencedaily.com/releases/2012/06/120605172013.htm

https://www.ncbi.nlm.nih.gov/pmc/articles/PMC3697075/

https://www.ncbi.nlm.nih.gov/pmc/articles/PMC3918007/

https://pcsp.libraries.rutgers.edu/index.php/pcsp/article/viewFile/2015/3424

https://thiswayup.org.au/how-we-can-help/internet-delivered-cognitive-behaviour-therapy/

https://web.archive.org/web/20121024054235/http://www.mindinbexley.org.uk/docs/E-self_help_guide.pdf

https://www.ncbi.nlm.nih.gov/pubmed/23746138

https://www.ncbi.nlm.nih.gov/pmc/articles/PMC4209079/

https://www.ncbi.nlm.nih.gov/pubmed/14622082

https://clinicaltrials.gov/ct2/show/NCT00769769

https://www.cambridge.org/core/journals/behavioural-and-cognitive-psychotherapy/article/multiple-access-points-and-levels-of-entry-maple-ensuring-choice-accessibility-and-equity-for-cbt-services/4E42E2795F93FCF6C8ECBE9B210BB0F0

https://www.psychologytoday.com/us/blog/think-act-be/201609/therapy-without-therapist

https://www.ncbi.nlm.nih.gov/pubmed/26302248

https://www.div12.org/dropping-out-of-cognitive-behavioral-therapy/

https://www.psychologytoday.com/us/blog/the-justice-and-responsibility-league/200903/four-drawbacks-cognitive-therapy

https://whywesuffer.com/tag/criticism-of-cbt/

https://www.ncbi.nlm.nih.gov/pmc/articles/PMC3673298/

https://www.nhs.uk/conditions/cognitive-behavioural-therapy-cbt/

https://digest.bps.org.uk/2018/08/13/interviews-with-100-cbt-therapists-reveal-43-per-cent-of-clients-experience-unwanted-side-effects-from-therapy/

http://www.thecbtclinic.com/pros-cons-of-cbt-therapy

http://www.thecbtclinic.com/the-cbt-treatment-overview

https://www.freeatlasthypnosis.com/benefits-criticisms-of-cognitive-behavioral-therapy/#

https://www.ncbi.nlm.nih.gov/pubmed/21458405

https://www.ncbi.nlm.nih.gov/pubmed/20599130

https://www.helpguide.org/articles/anxiety/therapy-for-anxiety-disorders.htm

https://www.ncbi.nlm.nih.gov/pmc/articles/PMC2789341/

https://learn.problemgambling.ca/eip/cognitive-behavioural-therapy

https://learn.problemgambling.ca/eip/inventory-of-gambling-situations

https://www.ncbi.nlm.nih.gov/pmc/articles/PMC4154573/

https://www.ncbi.nlm.nih.gov/pubmed/17927535

https://journals.sagepub.com/doi/abs/10.1177/0002764204270278

https://www.intechopen.com/books/cognitive-behavioral-therapy-and-clinical-applications/internet-addiction-and-cognitive-behavioral-therapy

https://connect.springerpub.com/content/sgrjcp/25/4/304?implicit-login=true

www.ingramcontent.com/pod-product-compliance
Lightning Source LLC
Chambersburg PA
CBHW060518290526
45791CB00001B/436